Oxford SKILLS WORLD
Listening
with Speaking
4

Katie Foufouti

OXFORD
UNIVERSITY PRESS

OXFORD
UNIVERSITY PRESS

198 Madison Avenue
New York, NY 10016 USA

Great Clarendon Street, Oxford, OX2 6DP, United Kingdom

Oxford University Press is a department of the University of Oxford.
It furthers the University's objective of excellence in research, scholarship,
and education by publishing worldwide. Oxford is a registered trade
mark of Oxford University Press in the UK and in certain other countries

ACKNOWLEDGMENTS

Cover illustration and main character illustrations by: Shane McGowan/The Organisation
Cover photograph: Hero Image Inc/Alamy
Back cover photograph: Oxford University Press building/David Fisher

Student Book

Illustrations by: David Arumi/Astound US pp.44, 58, 68; Valentina Belloni/MB Artists
pp.51, 53, 71; Robin Boyer/Illustration Online pp.40–41, 43, 82, 85; Mattia Cerato/MB
Artists pp.78–79, 81; Peter Francis/MB Artists pp.8, 26–27, 29; Angie Jones pp.32, 72;
Anthony Lewis/MB Artists pp.13, 15, 54, 64; Margeaux Lucas/MB Artists p.36; Juan
Moreno/MB Artists pp.11–12, 25, 50–51; Christos Skaltsas/Advocate Art pp.16, 30, 65,
67, 86; Jomike Tejido/MB Artists pp.22, 39, 57, 69

*The Publishers would like to thank the following for their kind permission to reproduce
photographs and other copyright material:* 123rf: 12 (river/Юлия Кузенкова), 14 (1a river/
Юлия Кузенкова), (2a island/Tatiana Popova), 26 (chess/Ip.2studio), 36 (young and
old people/Ian Allenden), 38 (a boys forehead/Eakachai Leesin), 40 (making jewelry/
Andrey Cherkasov), 42 (2a making jewelry/Andrey Cherkasov), 48 (earth from
space/Johan Swanepoel), 56 (4a star/Martijn Mulder), 66 (film set/Lothar Steiner),
68 (cartoon cat/jpegwiz), 70 (cartoon cat/jpegwiz), (cartoon sheep/Anna Kvach),
78 (crossroads/unicusx), (white van/vitpho), 80 (crossroads/vincentstthomas),
82 (farm/Maciej Maksymowicz), 88 (toy motorbike/Alberto Giacomazzi); Alamy:
6 (camels in desert/Norbert Eisele-Hein/imageBROKER), 20 (trampoline park/
Spencer Grant), 26 (jog/Martin Barraud/OJO Images Ltd), (surf/Jennika Argent),
(trophy/Image Source Plus), 28 (4a trophy/Image Source Plus), (4b surfing/Jennika
Argent), 36 (eyebrows and eye/Rayon), 38 (d girls face/Hero Image Inc.), 64 (boy
watching tv/Image Source); Getty: 22 (play golf/Blend Images–Erik Isakson),
24 (golf/blackred), (tennis/Andriy Onufriyenko), 28 (1b chess/kate_sept2004),
37 (man and woman kitchen/Hero Images), 38 (c arm/Westend61), 40 (haircut/Don
Mason), 42 (2b haircut/Don Mason), 46 (three children/JGI/Jamie Grill), 54 (dream/
PM Images), 55 (girl with telescope/blue jeans images), 64 (newsdesk/simonkr),
69 (two people watching tv/Tetra Images); Oxford University Press: 10 (c. canyon/
Shutterstock; sumikophoto), 12 (cave/Shutterstock/kaetana), (cliff/Shutterstock/
Krikkiat), (waterfall/Shutterstock/Galyna Andrushko), 14 (2b cave/Shutterstock/
Krikkiat), (3b cliffs/Shutterstock/Adrian Reynolds), (4b waterfall/Shutterstock/Galyna
Andrushko), 22 (table tennis/Shutterstock), 36 (crying/Shutterstock/Zdorov Kirill
Vladimirovich), 40 (earrings/Shutterstock/AleksandrN), 42 (1b earrings/Shutterstock/
AleksandrN), 50 (planet/Shutterstock/Tristan3D), 52 (planet/Shutterstock/Ksanawo),
54 (satellite/123rf/abidal), 56 (2b satellite/Shutterstock/Andrey Armyagov), 68 (lion/
Shutterstock; Maggy Meyer), 70 (elephants walking/Shutterstock/BlueSkyImage),
(lion/Shutterstock; Maggy Meyer), 78 (traffic lights/Shutterstock; AlinaStreltsova),
80 (tower block/Shutterstock/kampolz), 83 (traffic jam/Shutterstock/chungking),
84 (4b vegetables at market/Shutterstock/Baloncici); Shutterstock: 8 (canyon/
SAPhotog), (desert/Agatha Kadar), (oasis/photosounds), (pond/Bildagentur Zoonar
GmbH), (stream/Bildagentur Zoonar GmbH), (thermometer outside/Dora Zett), 9 (city
skyline cloudy/Monicami), (city skyline sunset/Cara-Foto), 10 (a. pond/kavram), (b.
desert/Vixit), (d. stream/Bildagentur Zoonar GmbH), 12 (canal/Alexpunker), (island/
Aleksei Kazachok), 14 (1b canal/Alexpunker), (3a waterfall/Maridav), (4a river/Robert
Crum), 18 (bridge over river/Orhan Cam), 22 (coach/Monkey Business Images), (play
tennis/Catalin Petolea), (play volleyball/dotshock), (tai chi/Katoosha), 23 (adult tai
chi/cowardlion), 24 (table tennis/muzsy), (volleyball/myone4u), 26 (gymnastics/
Dmytro Vietrov), (judo/BRG.photography), 28 (1a gymnastics/Dmytro Vietrov),
(2a judo/BRG.photography), (2b gymnastics/Nikolaeva Galina), (3a jogging/Daxiao
Productions), (3b surfing/Martin Charles Hatch), 34 (children smiling/Rawpixel.
com), 36 (dark hair/Africa Studio), (five arms/Luis Louro), (wavy hair/ZaZa Studio),
37 (girl and baby/fasphotographic), 38 (b womans forhead/DreamBig), 40 (angry/
LightField Studios), (braid/Yganko), (clever/Rob Marmion), 42 (1a girl plaits/In Green),
(3a angry/LightField Studios), (3b making jewelry/VladKK), (4a earrings/PrimePhoto),
(4b angry girl/Dean Drobot), 50 (footprint/Sharomka), (galaxy/Aphelleon), (ground/
Bernd Schmidt), (meteorite/christo mitkov christov), (plane landing/Senohrabek),
52 (footprint/George Dolgikh), (galaxy/muratart), (meteorite/Jiri Vaclavek),
54 (asteroid/Michal Zdunkiak), (moon/dimpank), (solar system/Sergey Nivens), (star
at night/Eliyahu Ungar-Sargon), 55 (astronaut in space/Marc Ward), 56 (1a asteroid/
Michal Zdunkiak), (1b moon/Ondrej Chvatal), (2a solar system/Sergey Nivens),
(3a start at night/Eliyahu Ungar-Sargon), (3b asteroid shower/Oliver Denker),
(4b moon/dimpank), 60 (moon in clouds/Zacarias Pereira da Mata), 62 (cinema/
Tompi), (end credits/Vector and Macrophoto), 64 (cameraperson/PHILIPIMAGE),
(car radio/LDWYTN), (directors chair and film/bioraven), (film poster/IAM
photography), 66 (camera man/Peter Kim), (news reporter/Leah-Anne Thompson),
(radio/Serggod), 68 (filming documentary/Maksimilian), (game show/Artisticco),
(person hiding behind hands/Marcos Mesa Sam Wordley), (science fiction/3000ad),
69 (girl blowing nose/My Agency), 70 (close up of eyes/Korionov), (filming
documentary/Maksimilian), (forzen land/Ewa Studio), (Science fiction/3000ad),
74 (taxi driver/Africa Studio), 76 (birds eye view road/TierneyMJ), 78 (person with
map/MilanMarkovic78), (tower block/Joe White), (traffic jam/egd), 80 (traffic
jam/bibiphoto), (traffic lights/Luis Santos), 82 (aerial view of town/Roschetzky
Photography), (blue truck/L Barnwell), (crowded place/Anton Gvozdikov), (lady with
vegetables/Rawpixel.com), (motornike/Mikbiz), 83 (farmers market/Rawpixel.com),
84 (1a aerial view of town/Roschetzky Photography), (1b crowded place/bivdone), (2a
motorbike/Jag_cz), (2b red truck/Ovu0ng), (3a motorbike/Mikbiz), (3b blue truck/L
Barnwell), (4a farm land/Ruud Morijn Photographer)

Workbook

Illustrations by: David Arumi/Astound US p.109; Valentina Belloni/MB Artists p.103;
Robin Boyer/Illustration Online p.113; Mattia Cerato/MB Artists p.101; Peter Francis/
MB Artists p.97; Angie Jones p.105; Anthony Lewis/MB Artists p.107; Margeaux
Lucas/MB Artists p.93; Jomike Tejido/MB Artists p.111

*The Publishers would like to thank the following for their kind permission to reproduce
photographs and other copyright material:* 123rf: 92 (3a river/Юлия Кузенкова), 94 (1a
island/Tatiana Popova), (1b river/Юлия Кузенкова), (3a river/Юлия Кузенкова), 98 (1a
playing chess/Ip.2studio), 100 (3b old and young women/Ian Allenden), 102 (1c
making jewelry/Andrey Cherkasov), 106 (3b star/Martijn Mulder), 108 (3a film set/
Lothar Steiner), 110 (1b cartoon ship/Anna Kvach), 112 (1a white van/vitpho), (3a
crossroads/unicusx), (4a crossroads/vincentstthomas), 114 (3c farm land/Maciej
Maksymowicz), 110 (2c cartoon cat/jpegwiz); Alamy: 95 (two women wathcing
tv/Tetra Images), 98 (2c jog/Martin Barraud/OJO Images Ltd), (3a surfing/Jennika
Argent), 100 (1a eyebrows/Rayon), (2a wavy hair/Hero Images Inc.), 108 (4a boy
watching telly/Image Source); Getty: 91 (running in canyon/kyletperry), 96 (1b
tennis racket/Andriy Onufriyenko), (3b golf club and ball/blackred), (4b playing
golf/Blend Images - Erik Isakson), 98 (3c plauig chess/kate_sept2004), 102 (2a
haircut/Don Mason), 106 (2c daydream/PM Images), 108 (1b newsdesk/simonkr);
Oxford University Press: 92 (3b canyon/Shutterstock; sumikophoto), (4b stream/
Shutterstock/Sergey Bogdanov), 94 (1c cliff/Shutterstock/Adrian Reynolds), (2b
cliff/Shutterstock/kaetana), (2c cave/Shutterstock/Krikkiat), 96 (2b table tennis/
Shutterstock), 100 (2b crying/Shutterstock/Zdorov Kirill Vladimirovich), 104 (1b
planet/Shutterstock/Tristan3D), 106 (1b satellite/123rf/abidal), 110 (1a lion/
Shutterstock; Maggy Meyer), (2a elephants/Shutterstock/BlueSkyImage), 112 (2a
tower block/Shutterstock/kampolz), (2b traffic lights/Shutterstock; AlinaStreltsova),
114 (1a vegetables/Shutterstock/Baloncici); Shutterstock: 91 (openwater swimming/
Stefan Holm), 92 (1a oasis/photosounds), (1b canyon/SAPhotog), (2a desrt/Agatha
Kadar), (2b pond/Bildagentur Zoonar GmbH), (4a thermometer/Dora Zett), 94 (2a
waterfall/Maridav), (3b canal/Alexpunker), (3c island/Aleksei Kazachok), 96 (1a coach/
Monkey Business Images), (2a tai chi/Katoosha), (3a volleyball/dotshock), (4a tenis/
Catalin Petolea), 98 (1b judo/BRG.photography), (1c gymnastics/Nikolaeva Galina),
(2a gymnastics/Dmytro Vietrov), (2b surfing/Martin Charles Hatch), (3b running/
Daxiao Productions), 99 (art gallery interior/TK Kurikawa), (zebra at zoo/Vladimir
Wrangel), 100 (1b dark hair/Africa Studio), (3a forehead/DreamBig), (4a wavy hair/
ZaZa Studio), (4b five arms/Sergey Nivens), 102 (1a plaits/In Green), (1b clever girl/
Rob Marmion), (2b angry girl/Dean Drobot), (2c earrings/PrimePhoto), (3a making
jewelry/VladKK), (3b angry boy/LightField Studios), (3c braid/Yganko), 104 (1a road/
Bernd Schmidt), (2a footprints/Sharomka), (2b meteorite/christo mitkov christov),
(3a galaxy/Aphelleon), (3b meteorite/Jiri Vaclavek), (4a galaxy/muratart), (4b plane
landing/Senohrabek), 106 (1a star/Eliyahu Ungar-Sargon), (1c asteroid/Michal
Zdunkiak), (2a solar system/Sergey Nivens), (2b moon/Ondrej Chvatal), (3a asteroid
shower/Oliver Denker), (3c moon/dimpank), 108 (1a camerperson/PHILIPIMAGE),
(2a directors chair and film/bioraven), (2b radio/Serggod), (3b reporter/Leah-
Anne Thompson), (4b movie poster/IAM photography), 110 (1c science fiction
scene/3000ad), (2b close of eyes/Korionov), (3a watching behind hands/Marcos
Mesa Sam Wordley), (3b making a documentary/Maksimilian), (3c game show/
Artisticco), 112 (1b trafic jam/egd), (3b traffic lights/Luis Santos), (4b woman with
map/MilanMarkovic78), 114 (1b aerial view of town/Roschetzky Photography), (1c
farm/Ruud Morijn Photographer), (2a blue truck/Maksim Toome), (2b woman with
vegetables/Rawpixel.com), (2c crowded place/IngridHS), (3a motorbike/MiloVad), (3b
red truck/Ovu0ng)

Table of Contents

Hi! I'm Olly.

Hi, I'm Molly!

Introduction

Welcome to Oxford Skills World

Oxford Skills World: Listening with Speaking is a flexible paired skills course that takes students on a journey toward independent learning, providing them with strategies and support to reach their goals.

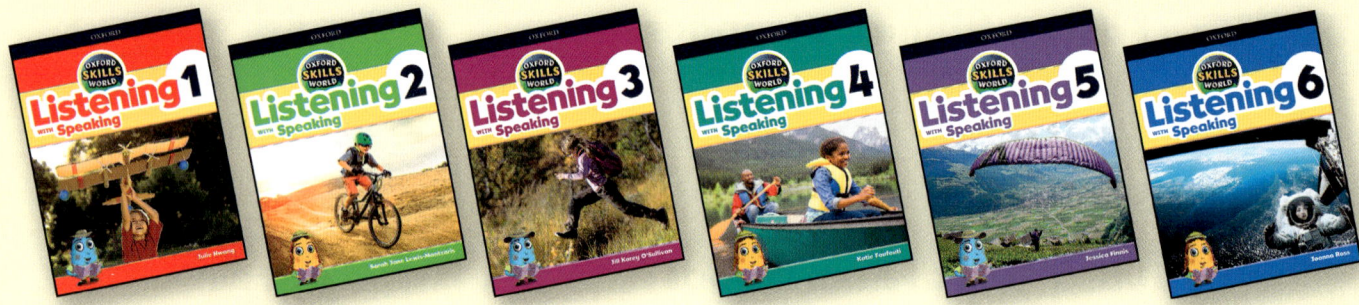

For Students

- Student Book / Workbook
- Student's website with downloadable audio and extra resources
  www.oup.com/elt/oxfordskillsworld

For Teachers

- Downloadable Teacher's Pack with instructional support, assessment, professional development videos, projects, and speaking resources
- Classroom Presentation Tool
- Teacher's website with downloadable audio and extra resources
  www.oup.com/elt/teacher/oxfordskillsworld

Be the Leader on Your Skills Adventure!

Hi! We're Olly and Molly, your skills adventure guides. We help you reach your goals by introducing new listening and speaking strategies, asking helpful questions, and giving friendly reminders. Most importantly, we cheer you on every step of the way! Let's go!

Quick Guide

Inside Each Topic

Topic Opener

Theme-based topics provide high-interest content relevant to students' lives.

My Goals introduces students to the objectives of each unit in the topic.*

Students listen to a Fun Fact to increase their engagement with the topic.

Fun characters, Olly and Molly, encourage 21st century skills like critical thinking, collaboration, and communication.

Students answer questions to activate prior knowledge and think critically.

Get Ready to Listen • Listen

Students learn and practice new vocabulary and complete the picture dictionary at the back of the book.

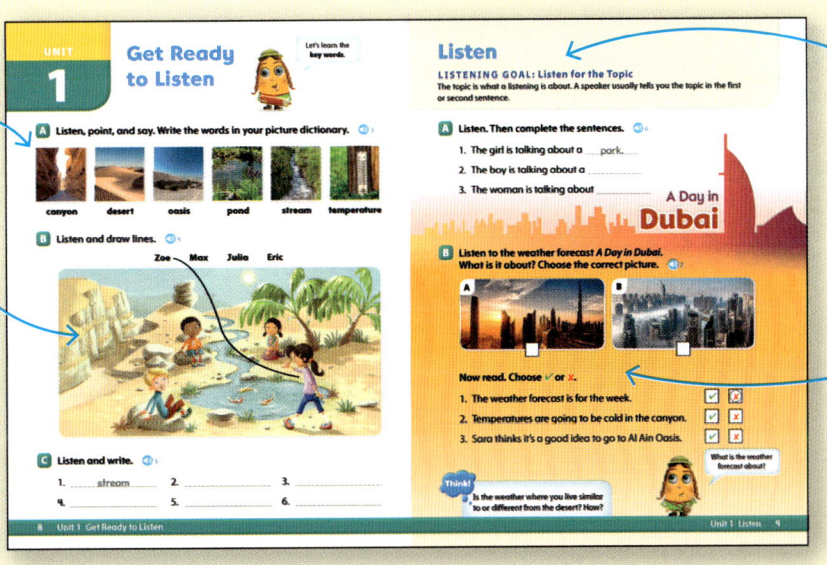

Listening Goals are strategies students can apply to any passage.

Students apply strategies to high-interest fiction and nonfiction passages, think critically about what they hear, and make connections to their own lives.

*Each topic contains two thematically related units.

Quick Guide

Understand

Students increase their comprehension of the passages by applying listening strategies they have learned.

Students complete activities to strengthen their understanding of the unit's vocabulary.

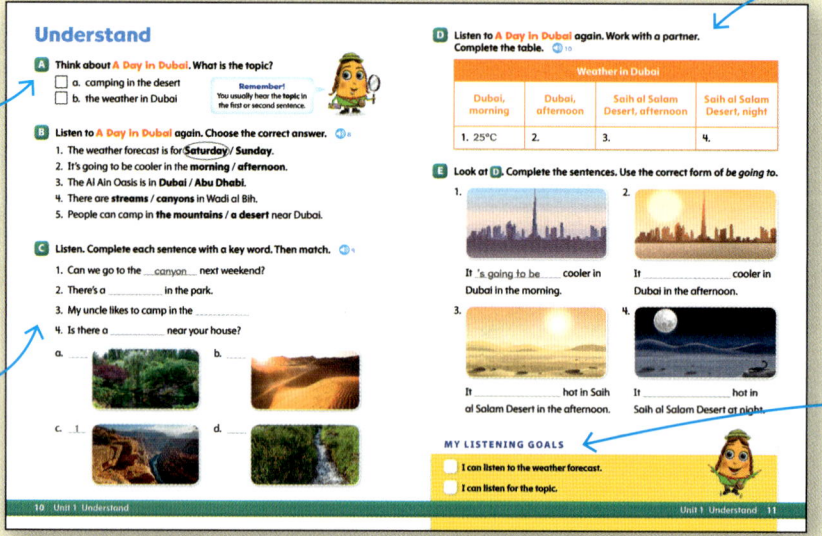

Students demonstrate comprehension of the unit's passage, vocabulary, and grammar.

At the end of each unit, students assess the progress they have made toward achieving their goals.

Listening Check

With helpful reminders from Olly and Molly, students apply the **Listening Goals** from both units to a new text.

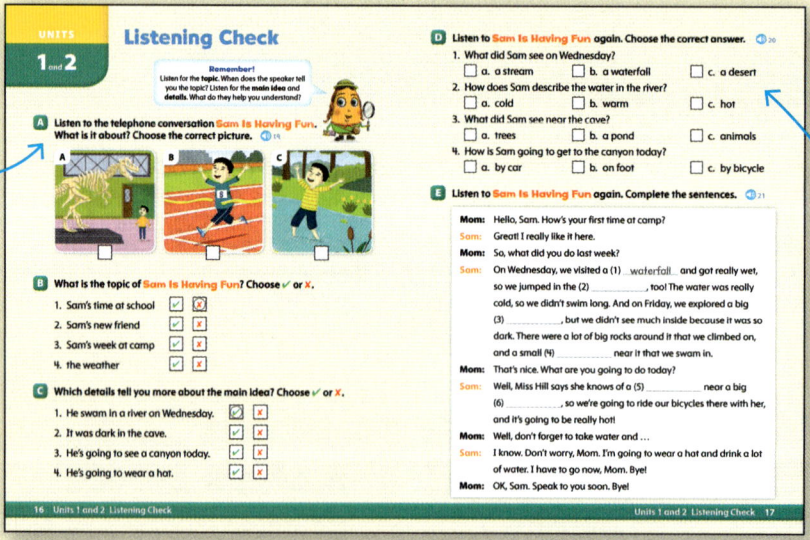

Students complete activities to boost listening comprehension and vocabulary application.

Get Ready to Speak • Speak

Speaking Goals prepare students to speak in different contexts.

Speaking Tips provide guidance on grammar, punctuation, and mechanics and help students speak fluently and accurately.

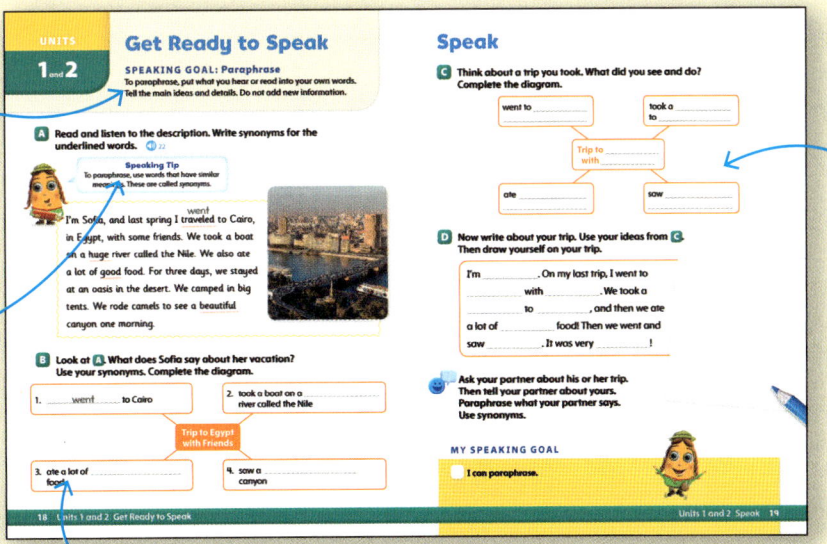

Scaffolded speaking models help students accomplish their speaking goals.

Students use graphic organizers to comprehend speaking models and to organize their thoughts for their own speaking.

Workbook

Workbook pages at the end of the book provide more opportunities for students to apply their **Listening Goals** and boost comprehension.

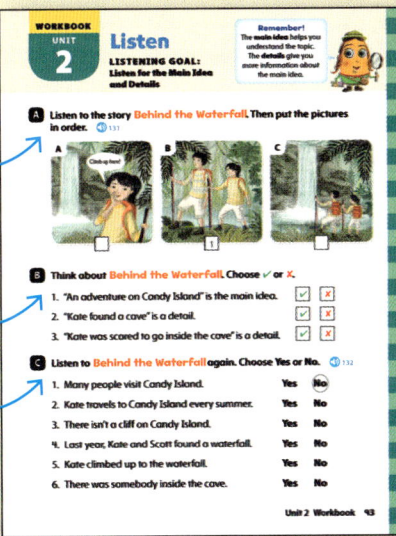

Additional activities provide extra opportunities for listening comprehension and vocabulary practice.

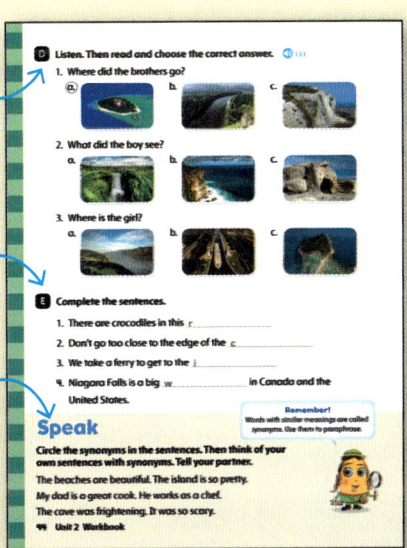

Students apply the topic's **Speaking Tip** to ensure proper usage in their own speaking.

Exploring Our World

MY GOALS

UNIT 1

- Listen to the weather forecast *A Day in Dubai*
- Listen for the topic

UNIT 2

- Listen to the story *Jerrie and Charlie*
- Listen for the main idea and details

SPEAK

- Paraphrase

A **Look at the picture. What do you see?**

1. Where are the people? What are they doing?

2. Do you want to go to this place? Why or why not?

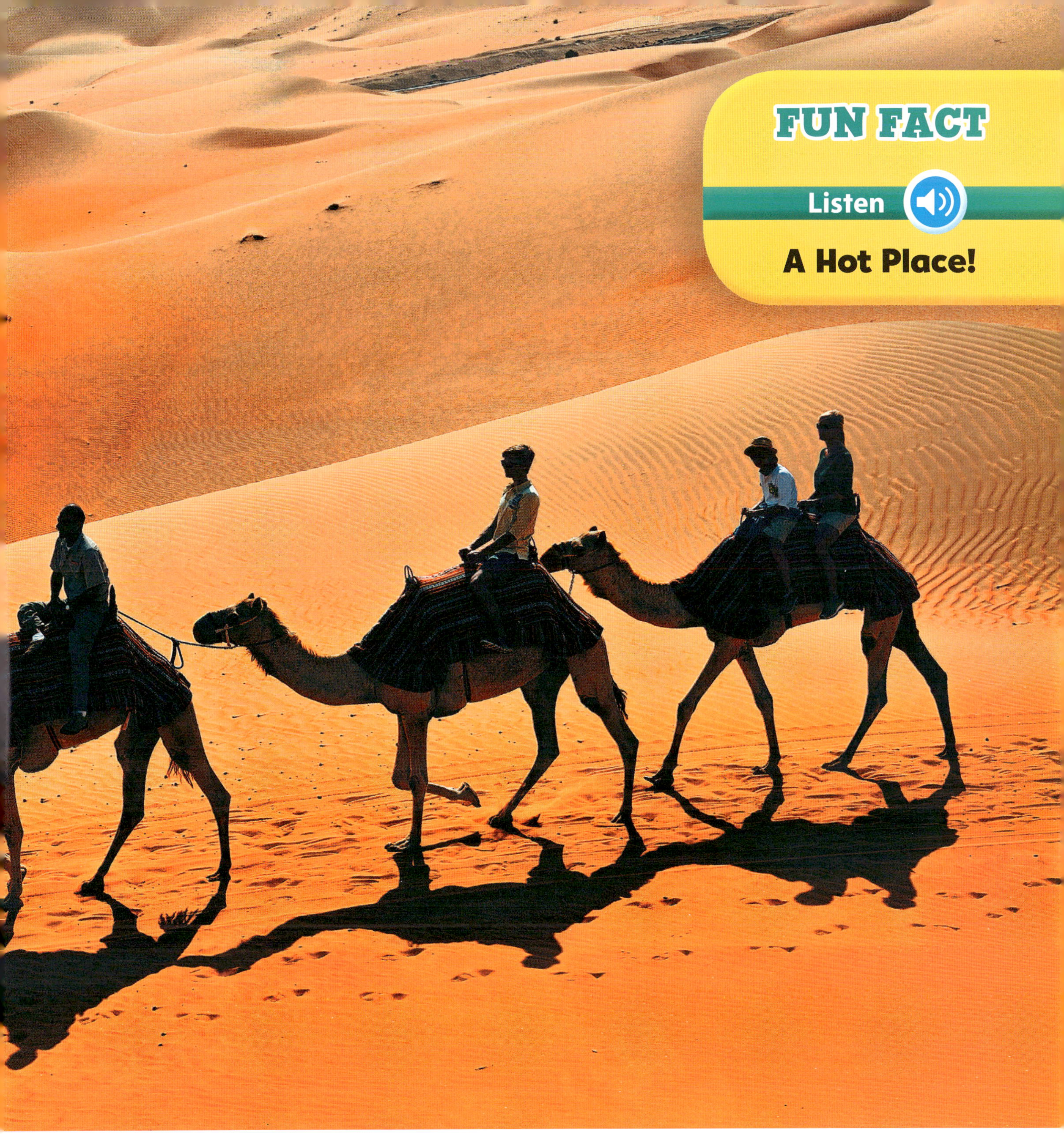

FUN FACT

Listen

A Hot Place!

B **Listen to the Fun Fact. Then answer the questions.** 2

1. How hot can it get in the Sahara?
2. Is the Sahara a good place for a vacation? Why or why not?

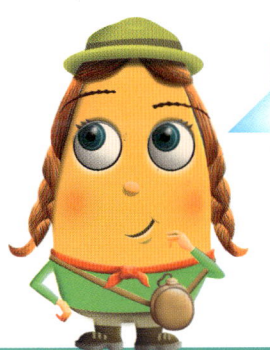

Think, Pair, Share
What's your favorite place? What can you see and do there?

Get Ready to Listen

Let's learn the **key words**.

A Listen, point, and say. Write the words in your picture dictionary. 3

canyon

desert

oasis

pond

stream

temperature

B Listen and draw lines. 4

Zoe   **Max**   **Julia**   **Eric**

C Listen and write. 5

1. _____stream_____   2. _____   3. _____

4. _____   5. _____   6. _____

Listen

A **Listen. Then complete the sentences.** 🔊 6

1. The girl is talking about a ____park.____

2. The boy is talking about a _____

3. The woman is talking about _____

A Day in Dubai

B **Listen to the weather forecast *A Day in Dubai*. What is it about? Choose the correct picture.** 🔊 7

A

B

Now read. Choose ✔ or ✘.

1. The weather forecast is for the week.

2. Temperatures are going to be cold in the canyon. ✔ ✘

3. Sara thinks it's a good idea to go to Al Ain Oasis. ✔ ✘

What is the weather forecast about?

Think!
Is the weather where you live similar to or different from the desert? How?

Understand

A Think about **A Day in Dubai**. What is the topic?

- ☐ a. camping in the desert
- ☐ b. the weather in Dubai

> **Remember!**
> You usually hear the **topic** in the first or second sentence.

B Listen to **A Day in Dubai** again. Choose the correct answer. 🔊 8

1. The weather forecast is for **Saturday** / **Sunday**.
2. It's going to be cooler in the **morning** / **afternoon**.
3. The Al Ain Oasis is in **Dubai** / **Abu Dhabi**.
4. There are **streams** / **canyons** in Wadi al Bih.
5. People can camp in **the mountains** / **a desert** near Dubai.

C Listen. Complete each sentence with a key word. Then match. 🔊 9

1. Can we go to the ___canyon___ next weekend?

2. There's a _____ in the park.

3. My uncle likes to camp in the _____

4. Is there a _____ near your house?

a. _____

b. _____

c. _1_

d. _____

D Listen to **A Day in Dubai** again. Work with a partner. Complete the table. 🔊 10

Weather in Dubai			
Dubai, morning	**Dubai, afternoon**	**Saih al Salam Desert, afternoon**	**Saih al Salam Desert, night**
1. 25°C	2.	3.	4.

E Look at **D**. Complete the sentences. Use the correct form of *be going to*.

1.

It 's going to be cooler in Dubai in the morning.

2.

It _____ cooler in Dubai in the afternoon.

3.

It _____ hot in Saih al Salam Desert in the afternoon.

4.

It _____ hot in Saih al Salam Desert at night.

MY LISTENING GOALS

☐ I can listen to the weather forecast.

☐ I can listen for the topic.

Get Ready to Listen

Let's learn the **key words**.

A Listen, point, and say. Write the words in your picture dictionary. 11

canal   cave   cliff   island   river   waterfall

B Listen and number. 12

C Listen and complete the sentences. 13

1. Can I take a photo of the ___waterfall?___

2. Do you want to go fishing in the _____ or the _____

3. You have to get a ticket to go inside the _____

4. From this _____, you can see a big _____

Listen

A Listen. Choose ✔ or ✘. 🔊 14

1.    ✔ ✘

2.    ✔ ✘

3.    ✔ ✘

B Listen to the story *Jerrie and Charlie*. What is it about? Choose the correct picture. 🔊 15

   **A**

   **B**

Now put the sentences in order.

a. Jerrie left from Ohio, USA.   `1`

b. Charlie nearly caught on fire.   ☐

c. Jerrie flew over caves.   ☐

What's the **main idea** and what are the **details**?

Think!
When was the last time you went on a trip? What did you see?

Understand

A Think about **Jerrie and Charlie**.
Are the sentences main ideas or details?
Choose **M** for main idea or **D** for detail.

1. Jerrie became famous for flying alone.   **M   D**

2. Jerrie's plane was named Charlie.   **M   D**

B Listen to **Jerrie and Charlie** again. Choose the correct answer.  16

1. Where did Jerrie fly?

☐ a. around the USA   ✔ b. around the world

2. How many times did Jerrie stop?

☐ a. 29 times   ☐ b. 36 times

3. What did Jerrie enjoy most?

☐ a. flying at night   ☐ b. flying in the day

C Listen and choose the correct picture. Then write the key word. 17

1.

2.

✔ a.   ☐ b.   ☐ a.   ☐ b.

river

3.

4.

☐ a.   ☐ b.   ☐ a.   ☐ b.

D Listen to **Jerrie and Charlie** again. Work with a partner. Complete the diagram. 🔊 18

1. Wh_y_____ → famous?

2. Wh_____ → start?

3. Wh_____ → see?

4. Wh_____ → favorite time?

E Look at **D**. Write the questions.

1.
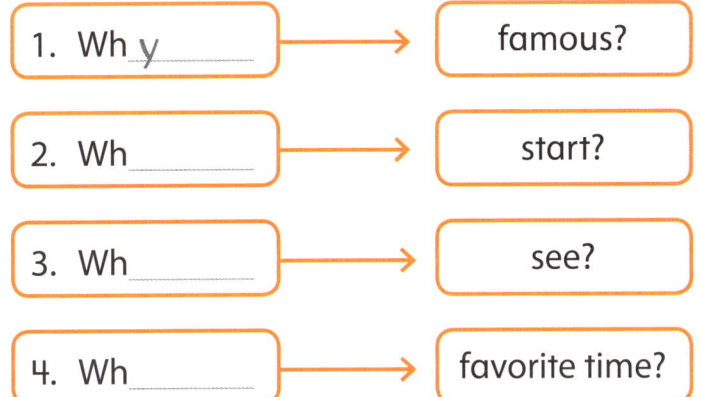

Why was Jerrie famous?

2.

_____

3.

_____

4.

_____

MY LISTENING GOALS

☐ I can listen to the story.

☐ I can listen for the main idea and details.

Listening Check

A Listen to the telephone conversation **Sam Is Having Fun**. What is it about? Choose the correct picture. 🔊 19

B What is the topic of **Sam Is Having Fun**? Choose ✔ or ✘.

1. Sam's time at school   ✔ ✘
2. Sam's new friend   ✔ ✘
3. Sam's week at camp   ✔ ✘
4. the weather   ✔ ✘

C Which details tell you more about the main idea? Choose ✔ or ✘.

1. He swam in a river on Wednesday.   ✔ ✘
2. It was dark in the cave.   ✔ ✘
3. He's going to see a canyon today.   ✔ ✘
4. He's going to wear a hat.   ✔ ✘

D Listen to **Sam Is Having Fun** again. Choose the correct answer. 🔊 20

1. What did Sam see on Wednesday?
   ☐ a. a stream   ☐ b. a waterfall   ☐ c. a desert

2. How does Sam describe the water in the river?
   ☐ a. cold   ☐ b. warm   ☐ c. hot

3. What did Sam see near the cave?
   ☐ a. trees   ☐ b. a pond   ☐ c. animals

4. How is Sam going to get to the canyon today?
   ☐ a. by car   ☐ b. on foot   ☐ c. by bicycle

E Listen to **Sam Is Having Fun** again. Complete the sentences. 🔊 21

Mom: Hello, Sam. How's your first time at camp?

Sam: Great! I really like it here.

Mom: So, what did you do last week?

Sam: On Wednesday, we visited a (1) __waterfall__ and got really wet, so we jumped in the (2) _____, too! The water was really cold, so we didn't swim long. And on Friday, we explored a big (3) _____, but we didn't see much inside because it was so dark. There were a lot of big rocks around it that we climbed on, and a small (4) _____ near it that we swam in.

Mom: That's nice. What are you going to do today?

Sam: Well, Miss Hill says she knows of a (5) _____ near a big (6) _____, so we're going to ride our bicycles there with her, and it's going to be really hot!

Mom: Well, don't forget to take water and …

Sam: I know. Don't worry, Mom. I'm going to wear a hat and drink a lot of water. I have to go now, Mom. Bye!

Mom: OK, Sam. Speak to you soon. Bye!

Get Ready to Speak

SPEAKING GOAL: Paraphrase

To paraphrase, put what you hear or read into your own words. Tell the main ideas and details. Do not add new information.

A **Read and listen to the description. Write synonyms for the underlined words.** 🔊 22

> **Speaking Tip**
> To paraphrase, use words that have similar meanings. These are called *synonyms*.

went

I'm Sofia, and last spring I traveled to Cairo, in Egypt, with some friends. We took a boat on a huge river called the Nile. We also ate a lot of good food. For three days, we stayed at an oasis in the desert. We camped in big tents. We rode camels to see a beautiful canyon one morning.

B **Look at A. What does Sofia say about her vacation? Use your synonyms. Complete the diagram.**

1. ____went____ to Cairo

2. took a boat on a _____ river called the Nile

Trip to Egypt with Friends

3. ate a lot of _____ _____ food

4. saw a _____ canyon

Speak

C Think about a trip you took. What did you see and do? Complete the diagram.

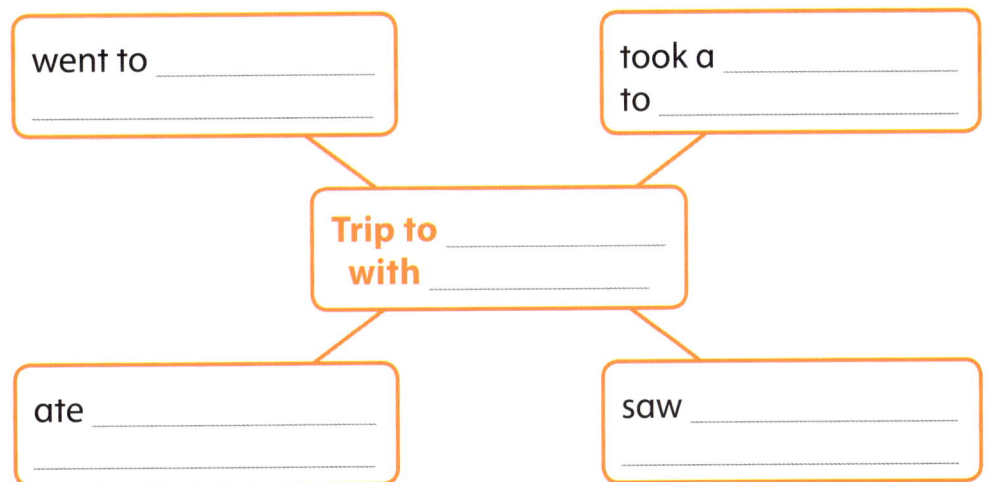

went to _____ _____

took a _____ to _____

Trip to _____ **with** _____

ate _____ _____

saw _____ _____

D Now write about your trip. Use your ideas from **C**. Then draw yourself on your trip.

I'm _____. On my last trip, I went to _____ with _____. We took a _____ to _____, and then we ate a lot of _____ food! Then we went and saw _____. It was very _____!

 Ask your partner about his or her trip. Then tell your partner about yours. Paraphrase what your partner says. Use synonyms.

MY SPEAKING GOAL

☐ I can paraphrase.

Faster, Higher, Stronger!

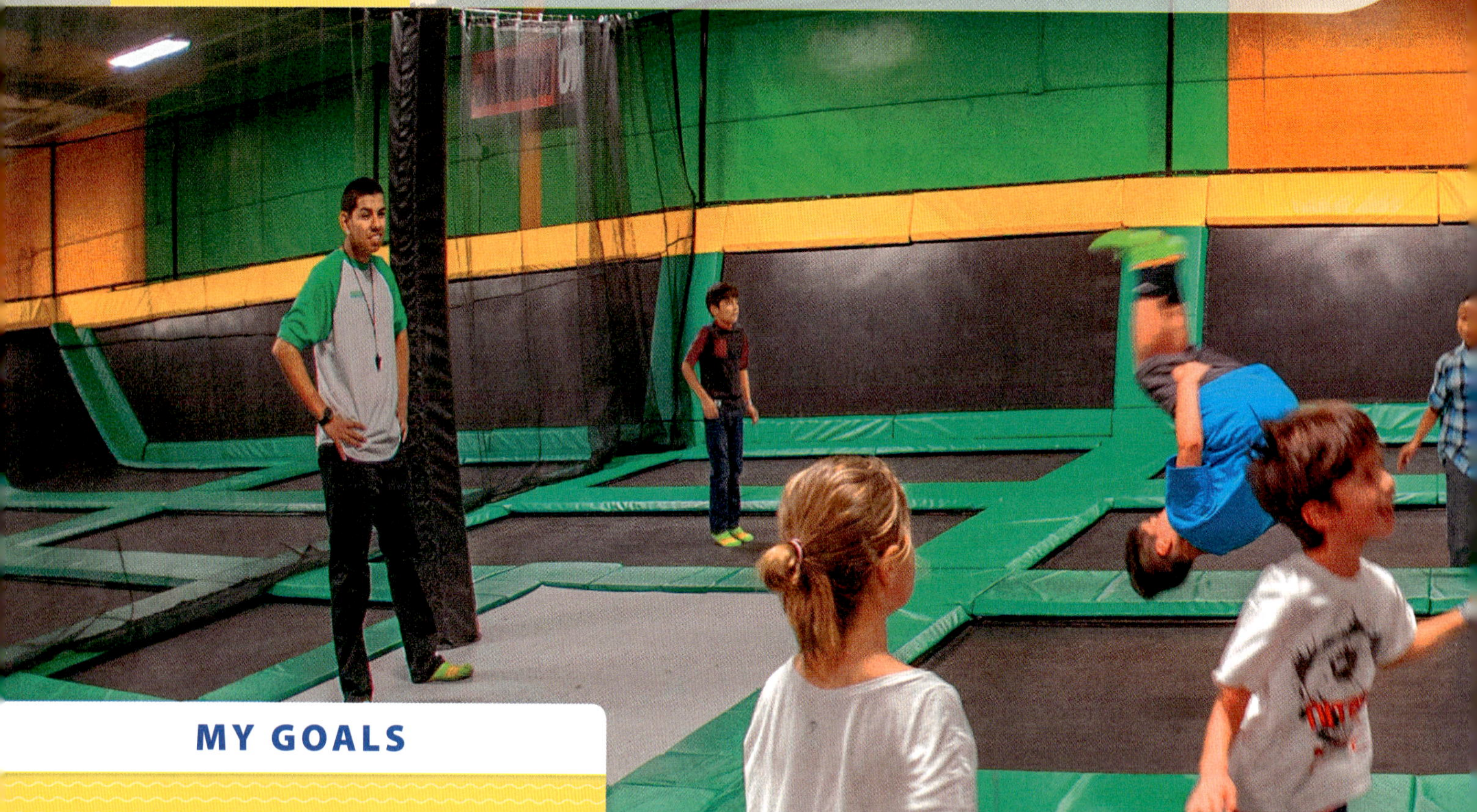

MY GOALS

UNIT 3

- Listen to the passage *Never Too Old for Sports*
- Listen and take notes — split page

UNIT 4

- Listen to the story *The Big Wave*
- Listen and make predictions

SPEAK

- Make predictions

 A **Look at the picture. What do you see?**

1. Where are they? What are they doing?
2. What types of exercise do you like to do?

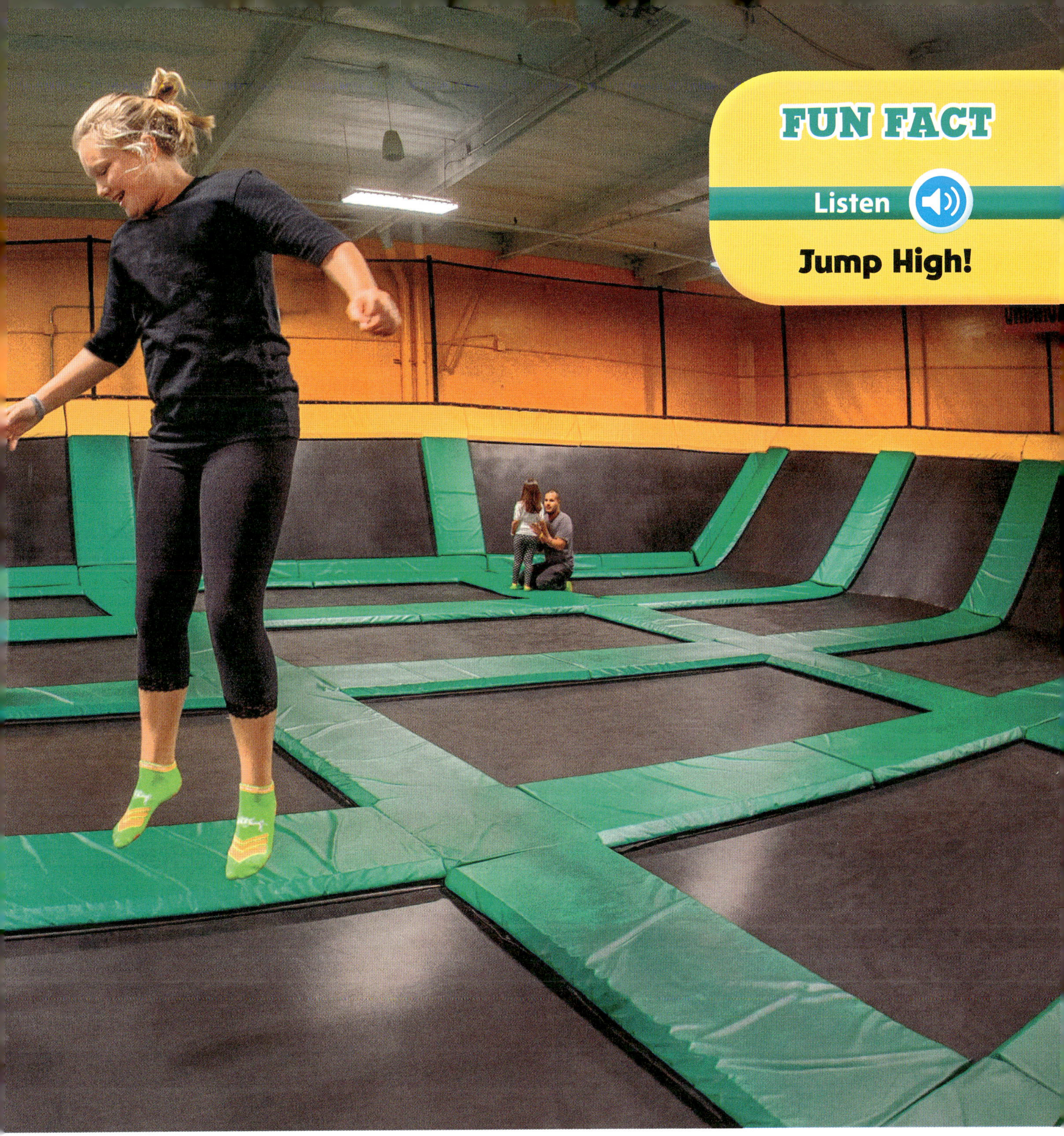

FUN FACT

Listen

Jump High!

B **Listen to the Fun Fact. Then answer the questions.** 23

1. Why is trampolining healthy?
2. Do you want to have a trampoline at home? Why or why not?

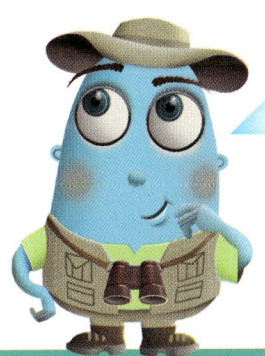

Think, Pair, Share
What is the hardest exercise to do? Why?

Get Ready to Listen

Let's learn the **key words**.

A Listen, point, and say. Write the words in your picture dictionary. 24

coach

play golf

play table tennis

play tennis

play volleyball

practice tai chi

B Listen and draw lines. 25

Maria   Chen   Emir   Mia

C Listen and write. 🔊 26

1. _____   2. _____   3. _____

4. _____   5. _____   6. _____

Listen

Split-page notes help you remember main ideas and details about them. On the left, write the main ideas. On the right, write the details for each main idea.

A Listen. Then complete the notes. 🔊 27

1. Ying   favorite sport: _____   lessons: _____

2. Tim   favorite sport: _____   plays at: _____

3. Laura   favorite sport: _____   practices with her: _____

Never Too Old for Sports

B Listen to the passage *Never Too Old for Sports*. What is it about? Take notes. 🔊 28

Main Ideas	Details
_____	_____
_____	_____
_____	_____
_____	_____

Now read. Choose ✔ or ✘.

1. The man works as a coach in a school.   ✔ ✘

2. He's talking about children and sports.   ✔ ✘

3. He's talking about people 70–90 years old.   ✔ ✘

What is an interesting **detail** in the passage?

Think!
What other sports are good for old people? Why?

Understand

Remember!
When you take **split-page notes**, write the main ideas on the left and the details on the right.

A Think about **Never Too Old for Sports**. Which sentence is a main idea? Which sentence is a detail? Choose **M** for main idea or **D** for detail.

1. Playing sports is good for old people.   **M** **D**

2. Old people like to play table tennis.   **M** **D**

B Listen to **Never Too Old for Sports** again. Choose the correct answer.  29

1. The coach works in a **sports center** / **school**.

2. Old people **don't like** / **like** to play sports.

3. Table tennis is **difficult** / **easy** because old people have to move fast.

4. The coach helps old people stay **tired** / **healthy**.

5. The coach's students play sports once or twice a **week** / **month**.

C Listen. Complete each sentence with a key word. Then match. 30

1. I like to _____ with my friend Alex.

2. At school, we _____ in gym class.

3. He _____ three times a week.

4. She likes to _____ on the weekend.

a. _____

b. _____

c. _____

d. _____

D Listen to **Never Too Old for Sports** again. Work with a partner. Complete the table. 🔊 31

Sports that old people like	Sports that old people don't like
1. golf	3.
tai chi	4.
2.	

E Look at **D**. Complete the sentences. Use (*don't*) *like to*.

1.

Old people <u>like to play golf.</u>

_____

2.

Old people _____

_____

3.

They _____

_____

4.

They _____

_____

MY LISTENING GOALS

☐ I can listen to the passage.

☐ I can listen and take notes on a split page.

Get Ready to Listen

Let's learn the **key words**.

A Listen, point, and say. Write the words in your picture dictionary. 32

| do gymnastics | do judo | jog | play chess | surf | win a trophy |

B Listen and number. 33

C Listen and complete the sentences. 34

1. I can't _____ or _____ today because it's raining.

2. Tom _____ at school. He's very good.

3. I _____ and I want to _____.

4. When does your brother _____

Listen

LISTENING GOAL: Listen and Make Predictions

A prediction is what you think is going to happen. When you listen, use clues to make predictions about how the story is going to continue and end. Clues can be what people say and do.

A **Listen. Choose the correct answer.** 🔊 35

1. The **red** / **blue** car is going to win.
2. It's going to **rain** / **be sunny** today.
3. She's going to **the park** / **take a nap**.

The Big Wave

B **Listen to the story *The Big Wave*. What is it about? Choose the correct picture.** 🔊 36

A

B

Now put the sentences in order.

a. Kekoa went under the water.

b. Kekoa was in the sea, waiting for a big wave.

c. Kekoa was riding a very tall wave.

> What do you think is going to happen next?

Think!

Which sports are dangerous? Why?

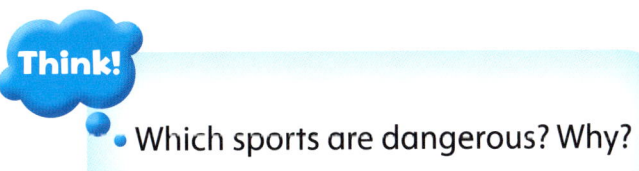

Understand

Remember!
Listen for clues to help you make **predictions** about the story.

A   **Think about The Big Wave. What clues helped you make a prediction? Choose Yes or No.**

    1. Kekoa went under the wave.   **Yes**   **No**

    2. They knew she was a strong swimmer.   **Yes**   **No**

B   **Listen to The Big Wave again. Choose the correct answer.** 🔊 37

    1. What sports competition is Kekoa in?

      ☐ a. World Surf Tournament   ☐ b. World Chess Tournament

    2. What else is Kekoa good at?

      ☐ a. doing gymnastics   ☐ b. doing judo

    3. The people were worried because Kekoa

      ☐ a. couldn't swim.   ☐ b. was under the water for too long.

C   **Listen and choose the correct picture. Then write the key word.** 🔊 38

1.   ☐ a.   ☐ b.   2.   ☐ a.   ☐ b.

3.   ☐ a.   ☐ b.   4.   ☐ a.   ☐ b.

D Listen to **The Big Wave** again. Work with a partner. Complete the diagram.  39

Main Idea

Kekoa isn't good at

1. _doing gymnastics_
2. _____

Kekoa is good at

3. _____
4. _____

E Look at **D**. Write. Use *is good at* or *isn't good at*.

1.

Kekoa _isn't good at doing gymnastics._

2.

Kekoa _____

3.

Kekoa _____

4.

Kekoa _____

MY LISTENING GOALS

☐ I can listen to the story.

☐ I can listen for clues to make predictions.

Listening Check

Remember!
Take **split-page notes**. What are the main ideas and details? Make **predictions**. What are people saying and doing?

A Listen to the story **Lots of Practice**. What is it about? Take notes. 🔊 40

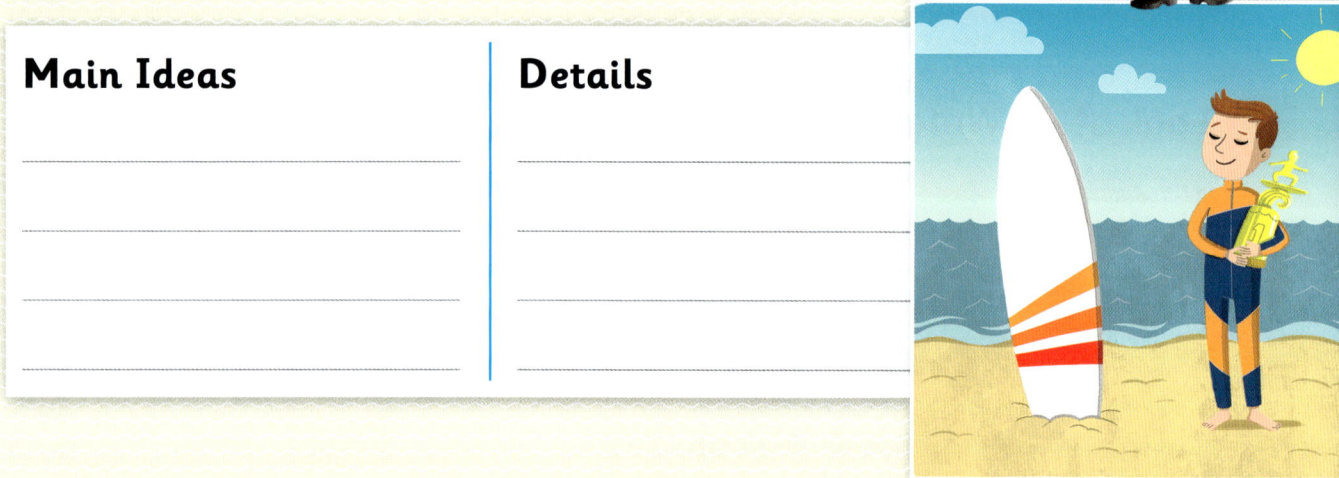

Main Ideas	Details

B Use your notes. Which sentences are main ideas? Which are details? Choose **M** for main idea or **D** for detail.

1. You have to practice when you don't want to.   **M   D**

2. It's hard to be great at a sport.   **M   D**

3. Robert likes to surf, and he practices a lot.   **M   D**

4. Five other surfers did better than Robert.   **M   D**

C What clues helped you make predictions? Choose ✔ or ✘.

1. Robert thought he was the best.   ✔ ✘

2. The tournament was in June.   ✔ ✘

3. He's much better now than he was last year.   ✔ ✘

4. I think he's going to win!   ✔ ✘

D Listen to **Lots of Practice** again. Choose the correct answer. 🔊 41

1. What do you have to do to win a trophy?
   ☐ a. eat a lot   ☐ b. sleep a lot   ☐ c. practice a lot

2. What sport does Robert like?
   ☐ a. surfing   ☐ b. golf   ☐ c. volleyball

3. When did Robert lose the surf competition?
   ☐ a. May   ☐ b. June   ☐ c. July

4. Why did Robert lose the competition?
   ☐ a. practiced too much   ☐ b. didn't feel well   ☐ c. didn't practice enough

5. When is Robert's next tournament?
   ☐ a. in two weeks   ☐ b. in one month   ☐ c. tomorrow

E Listen to **Lots of Practice** again. Complete the sentences. 🔊 42

It's hard to be great at a sport. It takes a lot of time and work to be the best. Do you want to (1) _____? Well, if you are going to (2) _____, (3) _____, or (4) _____, you are going to have to practice many hours every week to get one. Sometimes you have to practice even when you don't want to!

My friend Robert likes to (5) _____, and he practices a lot. Last year, Robert only surfed one or two times each month. He was in a surfing tournament in June, and he didn't do well. He thought he was the best, but five other surfers did better than Robert. His (6) _____ told him that he lost because he needed to practice more. Now he's surfing four times every week, and he's really great. He's much better now than he was last year. His next tournament is in a month, and I think he's going to win!

Get Ready to Speak

SPEAKING GOAL: Make Predictions

Predictions are things you think are going to happen. When you speak, use information you know to make predictions.

A Read and listen to the conversation. Underline the predictions. 43

Speaking Tip
Use *be going to* when you make predictions.

Ann: Hi! Do you want to watch a soccer game on Sunday?

Lisa: Maybe. Who's playing?

Ann: The Kites and the Wolves. They're both very good. Fernando plays for the Wolves, and he always scores. But the coach thinks he isn't going to play tomorrow because his knee hurts. Juan plays for the Kites, so I think they're going to win. It's going to be a great game!

Lisa: Let's watch it!

B Look at **A**. What does Ann say about the soccer game? Complete the diagram.

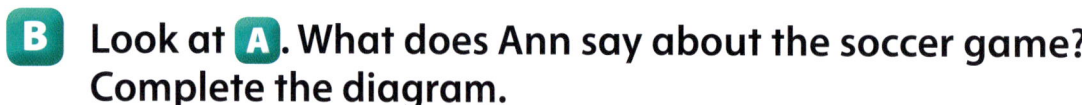

Teams	**Players**
1. the Kites and _____	2. _____ and _____

Soccer Game

Who's going to win?	**Watch or not watch?**
3. _____	4. _____

Speak

C Think about a game you might watch. Complete the diagram.

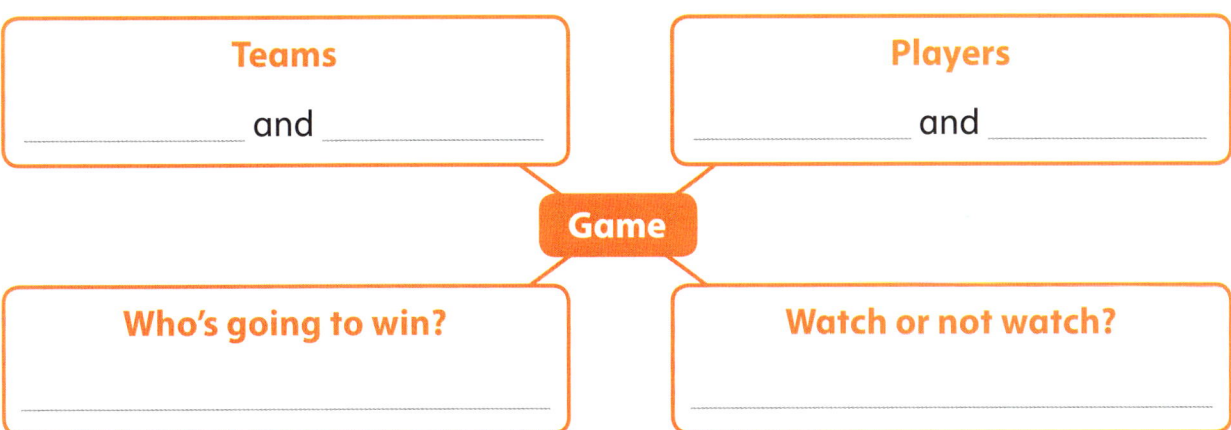

Teams	Players
_____ and _____	_____ and _____

Game

Who's going to win?	Watch or not watch?
_____	_____

D Now write your conversation. Use your predictions from **C**. Choose new words, too. Then draw your favorite player.

Me: Do you want to watch a
_____ on _____ ?

My partner: Maybe. Who's playing?

Me: _____ and _____ .

_____

I think _____
are going to win. It's going to
be _____ !

My partner: _____ !

 Practice your conversation with a partner and make predictions.

MY SPEAKING GOAL

☐ I can make predictions.

TOPIC 3

HEALTH

Look Good! Feel Good!

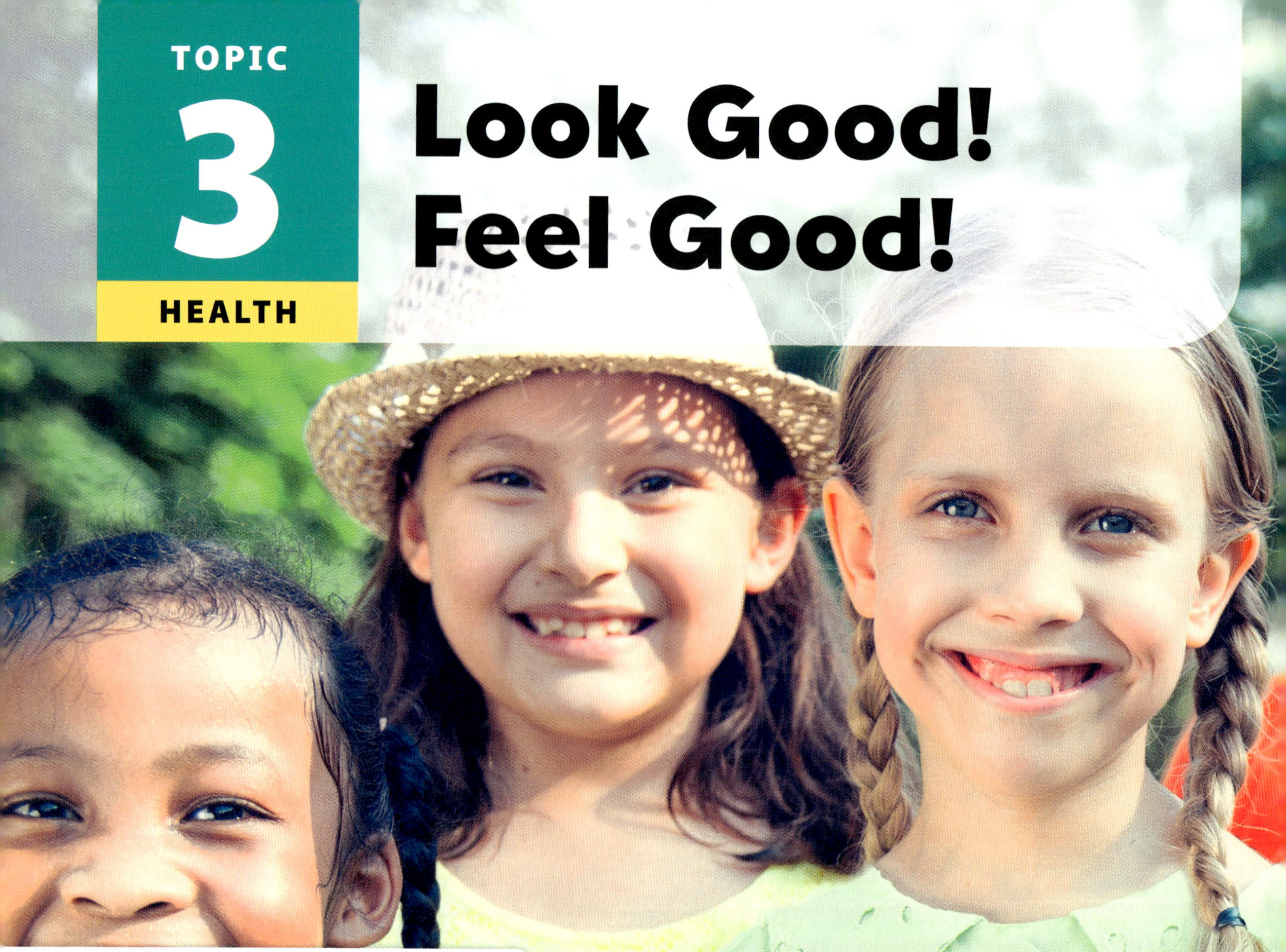

MY GOALS

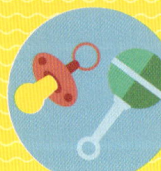

UNIT 5

- Listen to the conversation *My Family*
- Listen for facts and opinions

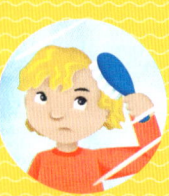

UNIT 6

- Listen to the story *The Hair Contest*
- Listen for plot

SPEAK

- Give and ask for opinions

A **Look at the picture. What do you see?**

1. What different types of hair can you see?
2. What type of hair do you and your family have?

FUN FACT

Listen 🔊

Let It Grow

B Listen to the Fun Fact. Then answer the questions. 🔊 44

1. How many hairs do blond people have?

2. How do you take care of your hair?

Think, Pair, Share
Is the way you look important? Why or why not?

Get Ready to Listen

Let's learn the **key words**.

A Listen, point, and say. Write the words in your picture dictionary. 45

| cry | dark | eyebrows | kind | skin | wavy hair |

B Listen and draw lines. 46

Jack   Grace   Jim   Lily

C Listen and write. 47

1. _____   2. _____   3. _____

4. _____   5. _____   6. _____

Listen

A Listen. Choose **Fact** or **Opinion.** 🔊 48

1. ☐ a. Fact ☐ b. Opinion
2. ☐ a. Fact ☐ b. Opinion
3. ☐ a. Fact ☐ b. Opinion

My Family

B Listen to the conversation *My Family*. Who is it about? Choose the correct picture. 🔊 49

A

B

Now read. Choose ✔ or ✘.

1. Peter has a sister and an older brother. ✔ ✘
2. Peter thinks his new sister is very pretty. ✔ ✘
3. The baby has the same kind of hair as Peter. ✔ ✘

Which information is a **fact** and which is Peter's **opinion**?

Think!
• Who looks similar in your family?

Understand

A Think about **My Family**.
Which is a fact?

☐ a. The baby doesn't have a name yet.

☐ b. Daisy is a nice name for the baby.

> **Remember!**
> A **fact** is something that is true. An **opinion** is what a person thinks.

B Listen to **My Family** again.
Choose the correct answer. 🔊 50

1. Mary is Peter's **sister** / **mother**.

2. The baby's eyes are **dark brown** / **blue**.

3. The new baby has very light **hair** / **eyebrows**.

4. The baby's hair is **straight** / **wavy**.

5. Peter **helps** / **doesn't help** take care of the baby.

C Listen. Complete each sentence with a key word. Then match. 🔊 51

1. Helen has beautiful, _____

2. She has brown eyes and dark _____

3. Does your brother have _____ eyes?

4. I have thin _____, like my dad.

a. _____

b. _____

c. _____

d. _____

D Listen to **My Family** again. Work with a partner. Complete the diagram. 🔊 52

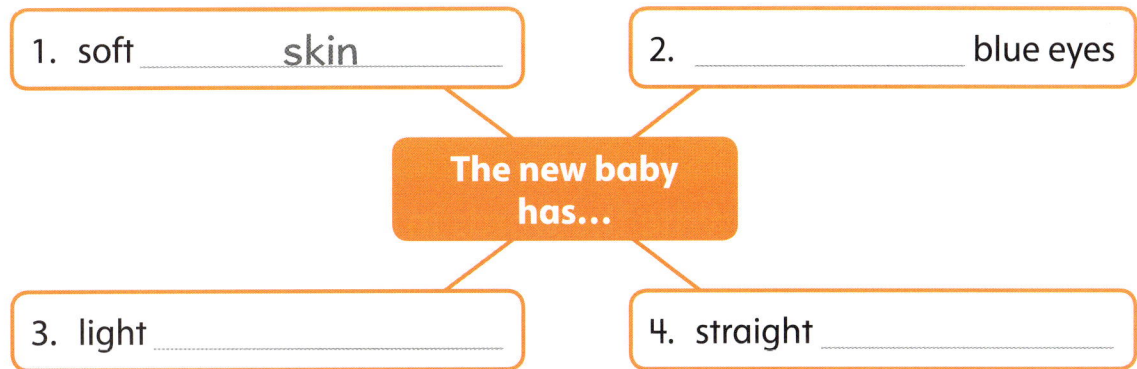

1. soft _____ skin _____

2. _____ blue eyes

The new baby has…

3. light _____

4. straight _____

E Look at **D**. Answer the questions. Use *does* and *doesn't*.

1.

Does she have soft skin?

_____ Yes, she does. _____

2.

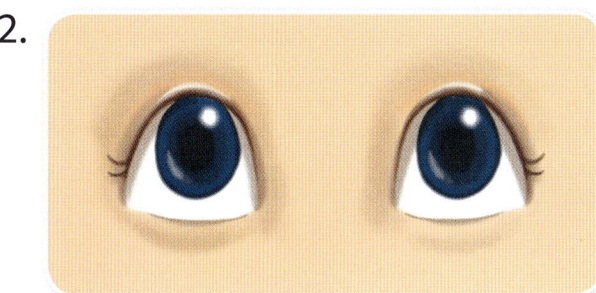

Does she have light blue eyes?

_____

3.

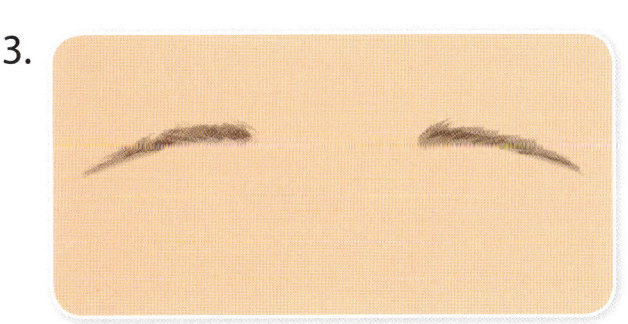

Does she have dark eyebrows?

_____

4.

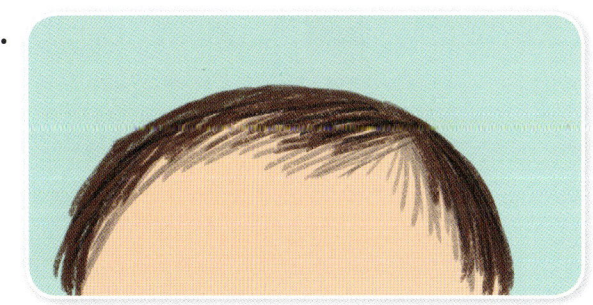

Does she have wavy hair?

_____

MY LISTENING GOALS

☐ I can listen to the conversation.

☐ I can listen for facts and opinions.

Get Ready to Listen

Let's learn the **key words**.

A Listen, point, and say. Write the words in your picture dictionary. 53

angry

braid

clever

earrings

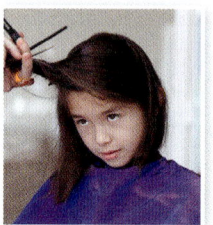
get a haircut

make jewelry

B Listen and number. 54

C Listen and complete the sentences. 55

1. Mary is _____ because someone took her _____

2. We _____ and sell it in this store.

3. The girl with _____ is very _____

4. I'm going to _____ on Saturday morning.

Listen

LISTENING GOAL: Listen for Plot

A plot has three parts. The beginning introduces the characters and setting. The middle introduces the problem and shows what happens. The end has the solution to the problem.

A Listen. Choose the correct answer. 🔊 56

1. The important characters of the story are a man and his **wife / daughter**.

2. The problem of the story is Mr. Silver loses a **pair of earrings / ring**.

3. At the end of the story, **Mr. Silver / Anna** finds the jewelry.

The Hair Contest

B Listen to the story *The Hair Contest*. Who is the main character? Choose the correct picture. 🔊 57

Now put the sentences in order.

a. Jeff talks to Alex about Elsa. ☐

b. Jeff brushes his hair. ☐

c. Jeff gets a text message. ☐

> What are the three parts of the **plot** in *The Hair Contest*?

Think!

• How often do you get your hair cut?

Understand

A Think about **The Hair Contest**. When do you learn about each thing? Choose **B** for beginning, **M** for middle, or **E** for end.

1. Jeff feels angry.   **B   M   E**
2. Jeff doesn't like his hair.   **B   M   E**
3. Jeff wins the contest.   **B   M   E**

> **Remember!**
> There are three parts to a **plot**: beginning, middle, and end.

B Listen to **The Hair Contest** again. Choose the correct answer. 🔊 58

1. Where is the hair contest?
   - ☐ a. on TV
   - ☐ b. at school
2. Why is Jeff angry?
   - ☐ a. He never wins prizes.
   - ☐ b. He won a math quiz.
3. Who makes cool jewelry?
   - ☐ a. Jeff's mom
   - ☐ b. Elsa's mom

C Listen and choose the correct picture. Then write the key word. 🔊 59

1.
   - ☐ a.
   - ☐ b.

2.
   - ☐ a.
   - ☐ b.

3.
   - ☐ a.
   - ☐ b.

4.
   - ☐ a.
   - ☐ b.

D Listen to **The Hair Contest** again. Work with a partner. Complete the diagram. 🔊 60

Cool Hair

Jeff
1. ___blond___ and
2. _____

Alex
3. short and
_____

Elsa
4. long and
_____

E Look at **D**. Answer the questions. Use *he's* or *she's*.

1.

Is Jeff the one with blond hair?

Yes, he's the one with blond hair.

2.

Is Jeff the one with straight hair?

_____

3.

Is Alex the one with long hair?

_____

4.

Is Elsa the one with dark hair?

_____

MY LISTENING GOALS

☐ I can listen to the story.

☐ I can listen for the plot.

Listening Check

A Listen to the story **The Wrong Haircut**. What is it about? Choose the correct picture. 61

A

B

C

B Which of the sentences are facts? Choose ✔ or ✘.

1. Kim had beautiful hair. ✔ ✘

2. Kim has dark, wavy hair. ✔ ✘

3. Kim went to get a haircut. ✔ ✘

4. Daisy's idea was very clever. ✔ ✘

C What happened in the plot? Choose ✔ or ✘.

1. First, Kim's friends got a haircut.   ✘

2. The problem was that Mrs. Scissors cut Kim's hair short.   ✘

3. Kim's friends found a solution to make Kim feel better.   ✘

4. At the end of the story, Kim still feels angry and sad.   ✘

D Listen to **The Wrong Haircut** again. Choose the correct answer. 🔊 62

1. Kim's hair was beautiful because it was
   - ☐ a. long and straight.
   - ☐ b. short and dark.
   - ☐ c. long and wavy.

2. What is Mrs. Scissors' job?
   - ☐ a. to cut people's hair
   - ☐ b. to make jewelry
   - ☐ c. to make clothes

3. Mrs. Scissors cut Kim's hair short because she
   - ☐ a. likes short hair better.
   - ☐ b. doesn't hear well.
   - ☐ c. doesn't see well.

4. How did Kim feel after getting a haircut?
   - ☐ a. angry
   - ☐ b. happy
   - ☐ c. tired

5. Kim's friends helped her feel better by getting the same
   - ☐ a. clothes.
   - ☐ b. haircut.
   - ☐ c. jewelry.

E Listen to **The Wrong Haircut** again. Complete the sentences. 🔊 63

Do you know Kim, that smart girl in my science class? She's the one with beautiful hair. It's long, (1) _____, and (2) _____. Well, last week, she went to see Mrs. Scissors at the beauty salon to (3) _____. "Please cut it just a little," Kim said. "Don't worry," Mrs. Scissors said. But Mrs. Scissors is really old, and she doesn't hear very well.

"Oh, no!" said Kim when she looked in the mirror. "It's too short!" Sad and (4) _____, she ran home and (5) _____ in her room all weekend. Her best friends, Lucy and Daisy, wanted to do something to help Kim feel better. Daisy had a (6) _____ idea, and she and Lucy went to see Mrs. Scissors. The next day, they went to Kim's house and rang the doorbell. Kim opened the door. "You have the same haircut as me!" she laughed. She felt happy to have such (7) _____ friends.

Get Ready to Speak

SPEAKING GOAL: Give and Ask for Opinions

To give an opinion, say what you think in a simple way. It's important to explain your opinions and to ask what other people think.

A **Read and listen to the conversation. Underline the opinion phrases.** 64

> **Speaking Tip**
> To give an opinion, use *I think* or *In my opinion*. To ask for someone's opinion, use *What do you think?*

Mateo: Look at the girl in the photo — the one with dark, wavy hair. I think she feels angry because her friends are using their phones. They aren't talking to her. What do you think?

Maria: In my opinion, she looks bored because she wants to watch a movie. Or maybe she wants to play outside, and her friends are making her wait.

B **Look at A. What reasons do the speakers give for their opinions? Complete the diagram.**

Girl with dark, wavy hair

angry because friends
1. using their _____
2. aren't _____ to her

bored because she wants to
3. watch a _____
4. _____ outside

Speak

C Work with a partner. Choose a topic. Write your opinion and reasons for it. Ask your partner for his or her opinion and reasons. Complete the diagram.

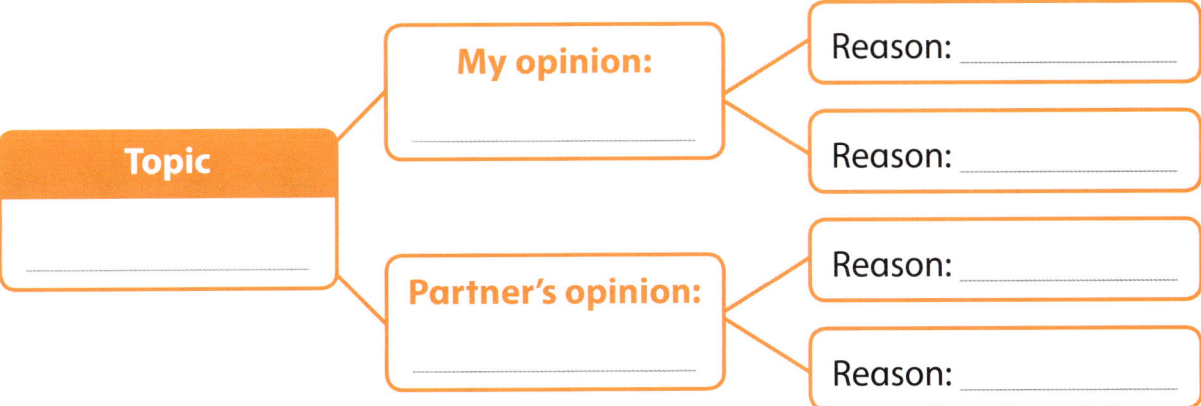

Topic _____

My opinion: _____

Reason: _____

Reason: _____

Partner's opinion: _____

Reason: _____

Reason: _____

D Now write your opinion. Use your ideas from **C**. Choose new words, too. Then write your partner's opinion. Draw a picture of your topic.

Me: I think _____ is _____ because _____ and _____ .
What do you think?

My partner: In my opinion, _____ is _____ because _____ and _____ .

 Do you agree with your partner's opinion and reasons? Tell your partner why or why not.

MY SPEAKING GOAL

☐ I can give and ask for opinions.

TOPIC
4
SCIENCE

What's Out There?

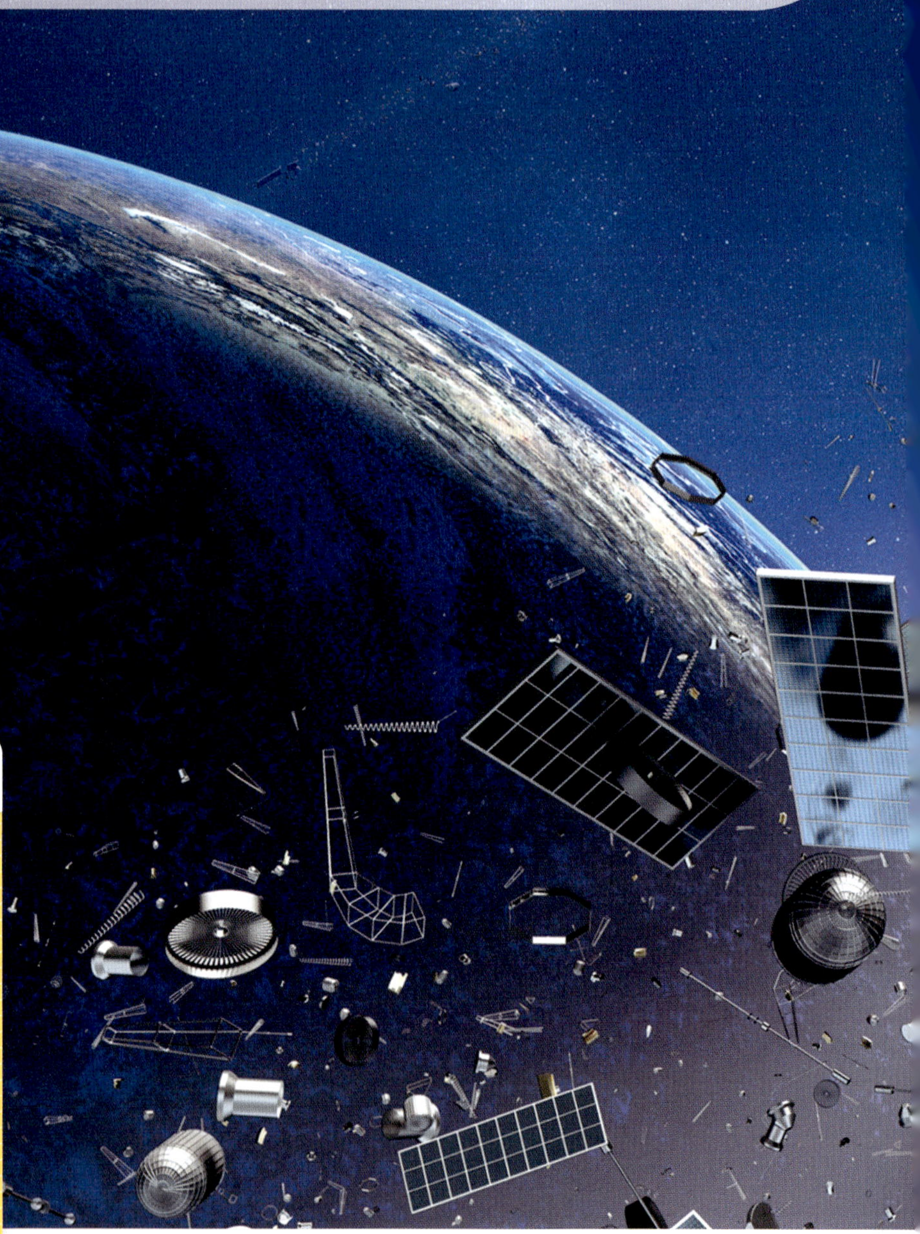

MY GOALS

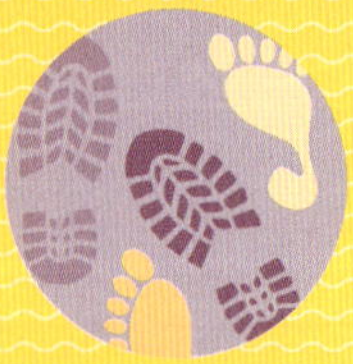

UNIT 7

- Listen to the story *They're Mine!*
- Listen for reactions

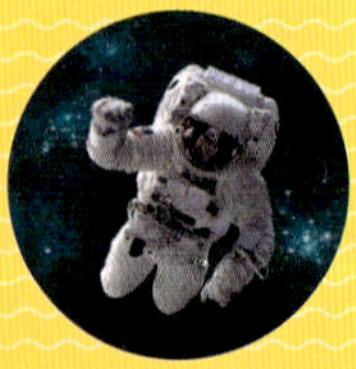

UNIT 8

- Listen to the class presentation *Erin's Dream*
- Listen for tone

SPEAK

- Use tones to react

A **Look at the picture. What do you see?**

1. What do you see? Where is it?
2. Are you worried about junk in space?

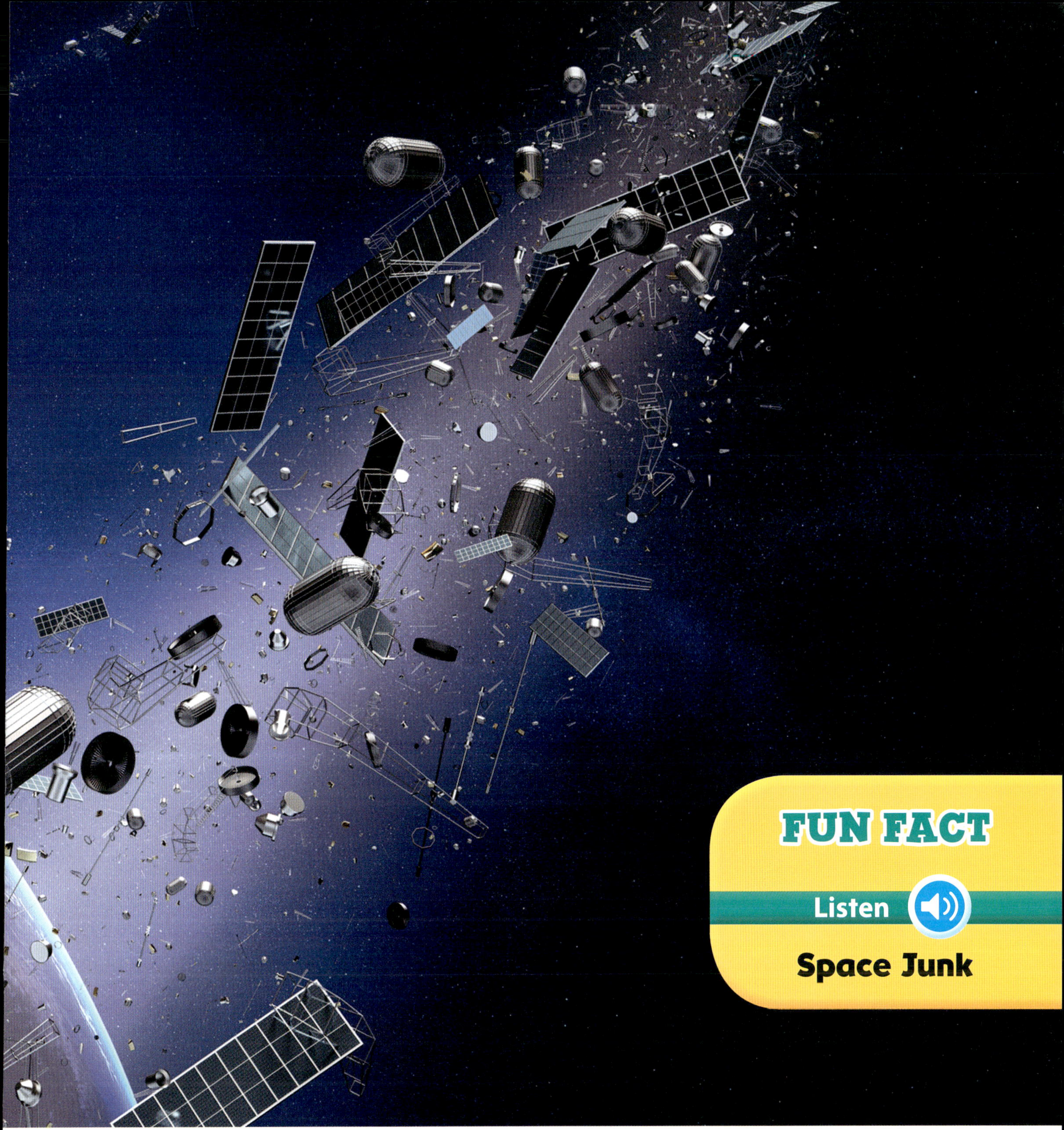

FUN FACT

Listen

Space Junk

B **Listen to the Fun Fact. Then answer the questions.** 65

1. How much junk is there in space?
2. How do you think we can keep space clean?

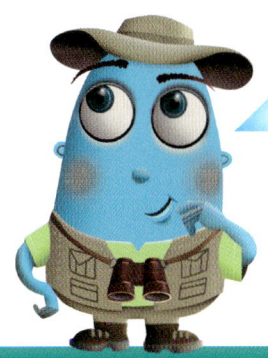

Think, Pair, Share
Do you want to travel to space? Why or why not?

Get Ready to Listen

Let's learn the **key words**.

A Listen, point, and say. Write the words in your picture dictionary. 66

footprint   **galaxy**   **ground**   **land**   **meteorite**   **planet**

B Listen and draw lines. 67

Lucy   **John**   **Mike**   **Rosa**

C Listen and write. 68

1. _____   2. _____   3. _____

4. _____   5. _____   6. _____

Listen

LISTENING GOAL: Listen for Reactions

A reaction is what a person does, says, or thinks after something happens.
Listen for reactions to know how a person feels and thinks.

A Listen. Choose ✔ or ✘. 🔊 69

1.

2.

3.

1. ✔ ✘

2. ✔   ✘

3. ✔   ✘

B Listen to the story *They're Mine!* What is it about?
Choose the correct picture. 🔊 70

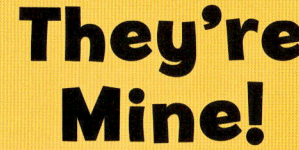
They're Mine!

A

B

Now put the sentences in order.

a. Jeong sees something on the ground. ☐

b. Jeong lands on another planet. ☐

c. Celia says they don't have much time. ☐

How did the astronauts feel when Jeong landed his spaceship?

Think!

• Why did Celia tell Jeong to be careful?

Understand

A Think about **They're Mine!** The astronauts say, "Good job!"
Why do they react this way?

Remember!
You can understand a person's **feelings** from his or her **reactions**.

- [ ] a. Jeong found a new planet.
- [ ] b. Jeong landed safely.

B Listen to **They're Mine!** again. Choose the correct answer. 🔊 71

1. Celia is inside **the spaceship** / **the space station**.
2. Celia and the other astronauts are usually **bored** / **busy**.
3. It was **easy** / **difficult** for Jeong to land on the planet.
4. Jeong finds some **footprints** / **boots** on the ground.
5. The footprints **are** / **aren't** Jeong's.

C Listen. Complete each sentence with a key word. Then match. 🔊 72

1. Our _____ is bigger than yours.
2. The astronauts are studying a _____
3. He found small _____
4. They want to explore a different _____

a. _____

b. _____

c. _____

d. _____

D Listen to **They're Mine!** again. Work with a partner. Complete the diagram. 🔊 73

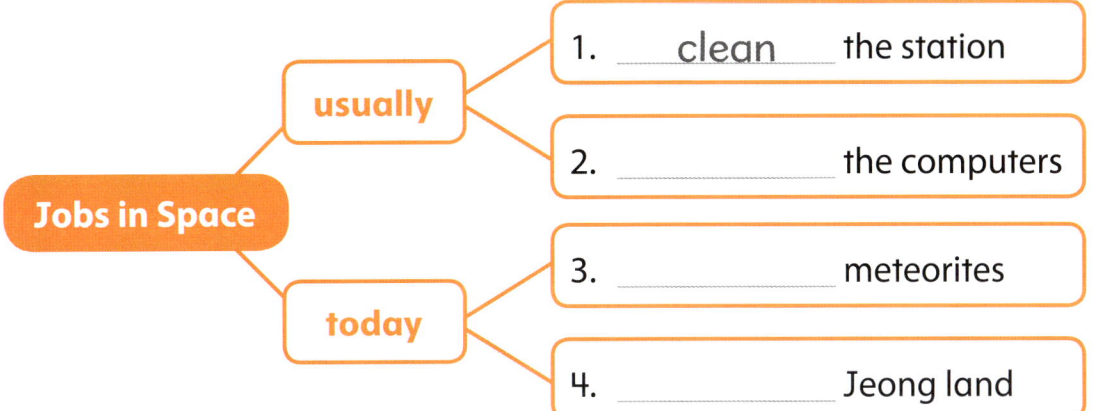

Jobs in Space

usually
1. _____clean_____ the station
2. _____ the computers

today
3. _____ meteorites
4. _____ Jeong land

E Look at **D**. Complete the sentences.

1.

The astronauts _usually clean_ _____ the space station.

2.

They _____ _____ the computers.

3.

The astronauts _____ _____ meteorites today.

4.

Today, they _____ Jeong land on another planet.

MY LISTENING GOALS

☐ I can listen to the story.

☐ I can listen for reactions.

Get Ready to Listen

Let's learn the **key words**.

A Listen, point, and say. Write the words in your picture dictionary.  74

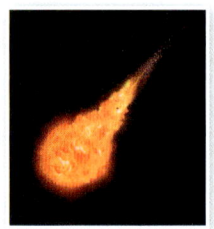

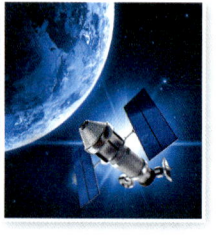

asteroid   **dream**   **moon**   **satellite**   **solar system**   **star**

B Listen and number.  75

C Listen and complete the sentences. 76

1. My _____ is to go to the _____ one day.

2. Is that a _____ or a _____?

3. Are there any _____ near Earth?

4. Our _____ is very big.

Listen

LISTENING GOAL: Listen for Tone

Tone is how a person talks: loudly, quietly, quickly, slowly. Listen for tone to know how a person feels.

A Listen. Choose the correct answer. 🔊 77

1. The man feels **tired** / **excited**.
2. The girl feels **bored** / **happy**.
3. The boy feels **sad** / **angry**.

B Listen to the class presentation *Erin's Dream*. What is it about? Choose the correct picture. 🔊 78

A

B

Now read. Choose ✔ or ✘.

1. Erin's dream is to travel on Earth. ✔ ✘
2. Erin can see stars and satellites. ✔ ✘
3. Erin doesn't like studying math. ✔ ✘

What do Erin's **tones** tell you about her feelings?

Think! Do you want to be an astronaut? Why or why not?

Understand

A Think about **Erin's Dream**. How does Erin feel? Choose **Yes** or **No**.

1. Erin is excited when she talks about space. **Yes** **No**
2. Erin is excited when she talks about math. **Yes** **No**

B Listen to **Erin's Dream** again. Choose the correct answer. 79

1. What does Erin want to be?
   ☐ a. a pilot   ☐ b. an astronaut
2. What can Erin see in the sky?
   ☐ a. satellites and asteroids   ☐ b. another solar system
3. What does Erin have to get better at?
   ☐ a. reading and gymnastics   ☐ b. math and science

C Listen and choose the correct picture. Then write the key word.  80

1.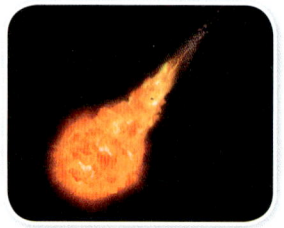
   ☐ a.   ☐ b.

2.
   ☐ a.   ☐ b.

3.
   ☐ a.   ☐ b.

4.
   ☐ a.   ☐ b.

 **Listen to Erin's Dream again. Work with a partner. Complete the diagram.** 🔊 81

1. go to _____ space _____

2. become an _____

Erin's Dream

3. travel around our _____

4. keep space _____

E **Look at** **D**. **What does Erin want to do when she's older? Write.**

1.

Erin _ wants to go to space. _

2.

She _____

3.

_____

_____

4.

_____

_____

MY LISTENING GOALS

☐ I can listen to the class presentation.

☐ I can listen for tone.

Listening Check

A Listen to the story **In the Schoolyard**. What is it about? Choose the correct picture. 🔊 82

B Think about the characters' reactions. Choose ✔ or ✘.

1. Mark's friends were angry when he flew too high.

2. They were happy because Mark came back.

3. They said "Wow!" because Mark's idea was bad.

4. They were surprised that Mark wants to go to Earth.

C Think about the characters' tone. Choose ✔ or ✘.

1. Jill was worried when she said, "Where is he?"

2. Ben isn't interested in Mark's dream.

3. Mark is sad when he's talking about his future.

4. Mark's friends want to hear about his dreams.

D Listen to **In the Schoolyard** again. Choose the correct answer. 🔊 83

1. What year is it in the story?
   - ☐ a. 2280
   - ☐ b. 2128
   - ☐ c. 2082

2. What is Mark good at?
   - ☐ a. scoring
   - ☐ b. kicking a ball
   - ☐ c. catching a ball

3. Mark's friends were worried because he flew too
   - ☐ a. slowly.
   - ☐ b. low.
   - ☐ c. high.

4. Where does Mark want to travel in the future?
   - ☐ a. Earth
   - ☐ b. in their solar system
   - ☐ c. around their planet

5. What does Mark want to study on Earth?
   - ☐ a. people
   - ☐ b. history
   - ☐ c. animals

E Listen to **In the Schoolyard** again. Complete the sentences. 🔊 84

On (1) _____ Latera, it's the year 2128. In a small town, the children are in the schoolyard. They usually play volleyboost in the schoolyard. Volleyboost is like volleyball, but the players ride on small rockets. Mark always scores because he can go really fast on his rocket. Once he rode it really high. "Where is he? Did he go to another (2) _____?" asked Jill. But then Mark (3) _____ softly on the (4) _____!

Today, the children aren't playing volleyboost. They're talking about their (5) _____ and what they want to do when they're older. "What do you want to do, Mark?" Ben asks. "My dream is to travel in space. I want to go to another (6) _____ and visit a planet called Earth," Mark says. "Wow! What's there? Tell us about it!" Mark's friends say. "People and animals lived there a long time ago, before we moved to Latera. I want to study its history."

Get Ready to Speak

SPEAKING GOAL: Use Tones to React

To show how you feel when you're talking, change the tone of your voice. Speak loudly, quietly, quickly, or slowly.

A Read and listen to the conversation. Underline Diego's reaction words. 🔊 85

> **Speaking Tip**
> Use reaction words to show how you feel. These are words like *wow*, *aw*, and *oh*. You say these more loudly, quietly, quickly, or slowly than other words.

Ana:	I won a photo contest!
Diego:	Wow, that's great! What did you take a picture of?
Ana:	I took a photo of the moon in clouds. Look. It's this one.
Diego:	Oh, that's beautiful! Did you win a prize?
Ana:	No, I didn't get a prize.
Diego:	Aw, that's too bad. Maybe next time!

B Look at **A**. What does Ana say and how does Diego react? Complete the diagram.

Story   **Reactions**

1. I _____ a _____ contest! → 2. Wow, that's _____

3. I took a _____ of the _____ → 4. _____, that's _____

5. I _____ get a prize. → 6. _____, that's too bad. Maybe next _____

Speak

C Think about an interesting story that a friend told you. Complete the diagram with what happened and how you reacted.

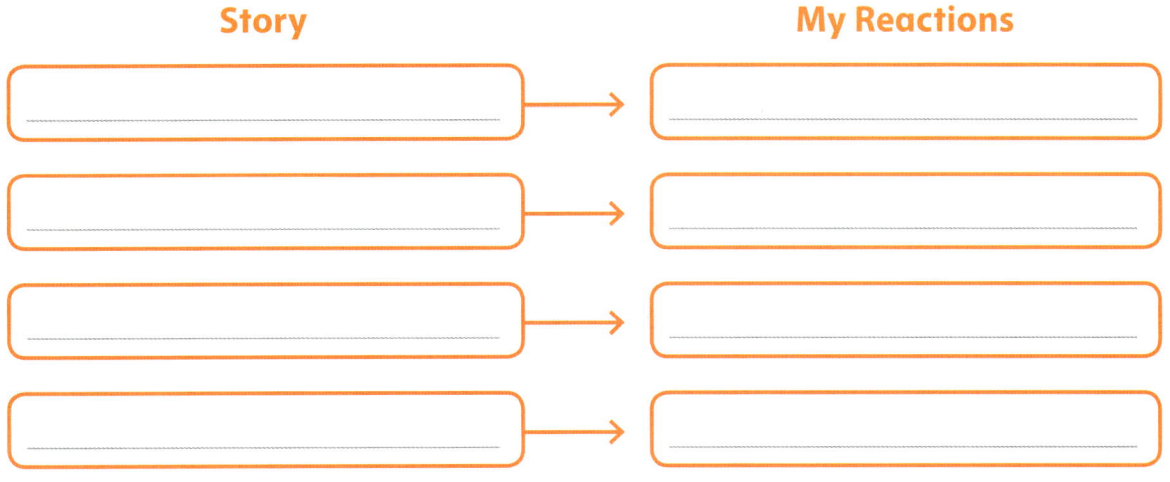

Story	My Reactions

D Now write the story. Use your ideas from **C**. Choose new words, too. Then draw a picture of the story.

 Tell your partner your story. Does he or she react the same way you did? Then listen to your partner's story and react.

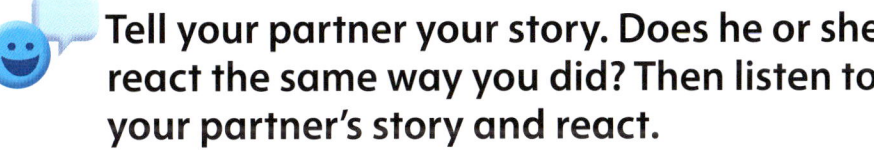

MY SPEAKING GOAL

☐ I can use tones to react.

The

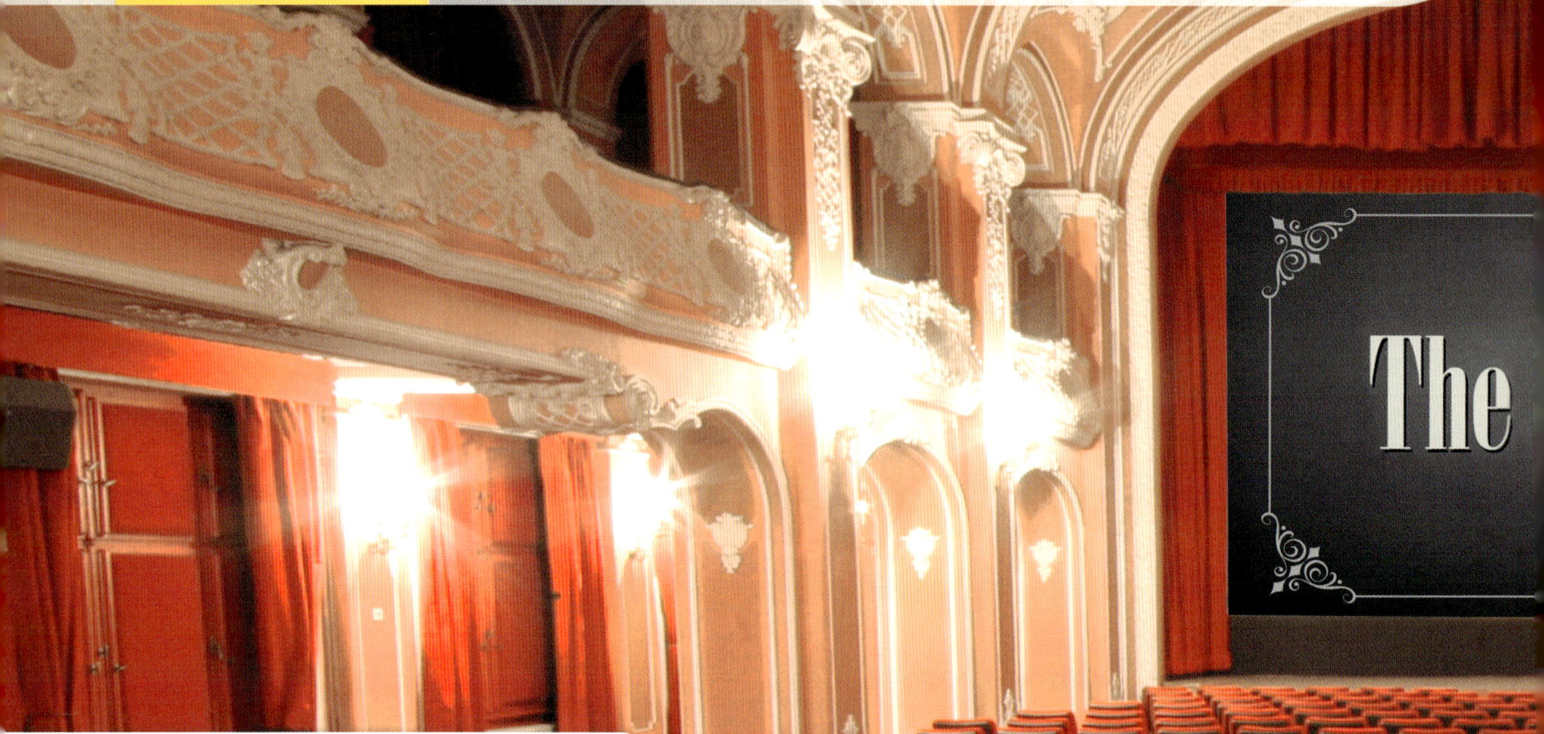

MY GOALS

UNIT 9

- Listen to the story *Clearview Park*
- Listen for unknown words

UNIT 10

- Listen to the conversation *The Weekend*
- Listen for definitions

SPEAK

- Give a review

A **Look at the picture. What do you see?**

1. How old do you think this movie theater is?

2. Are movie theaters today similar? Why or why not?

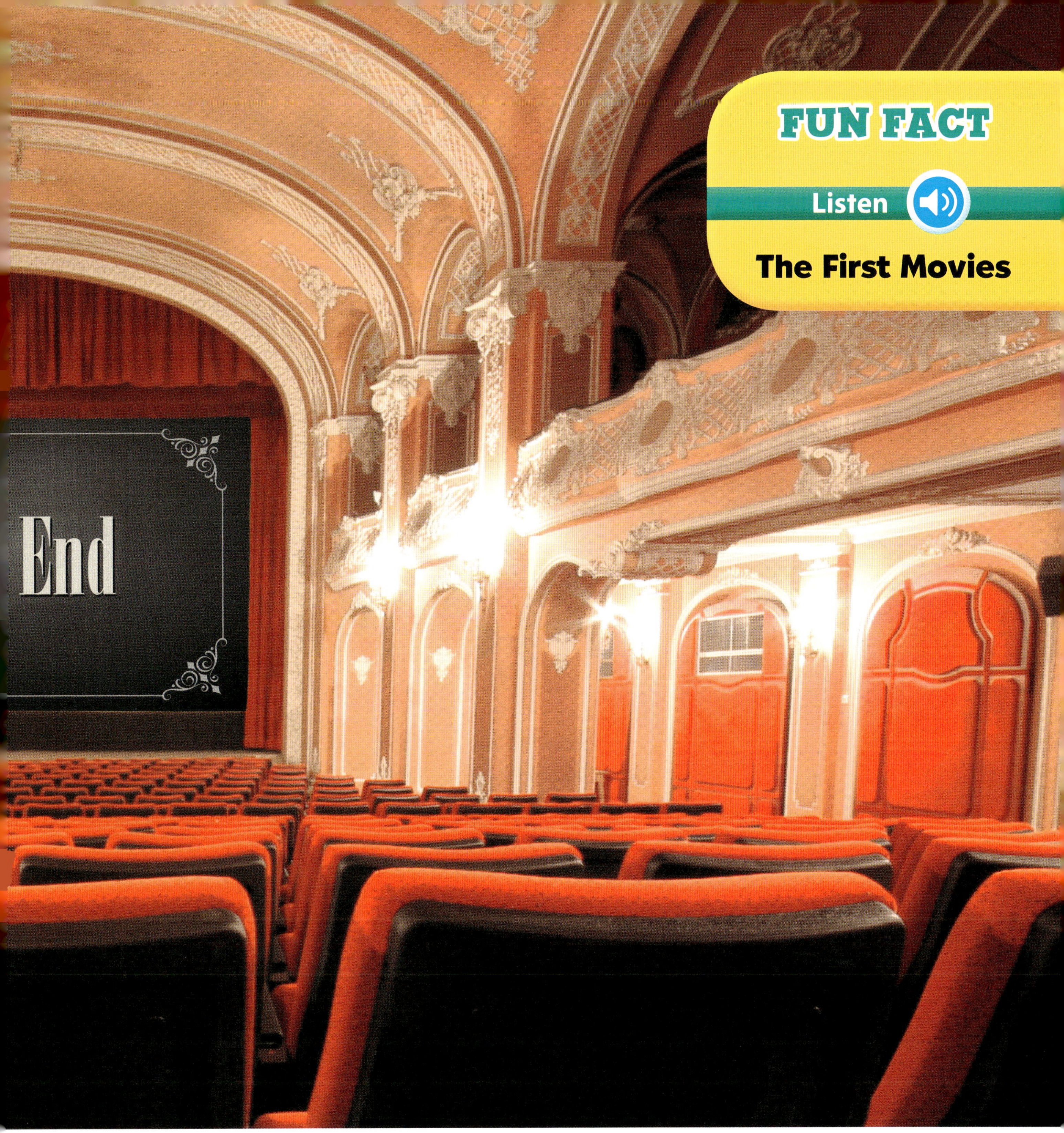

End

B Listen to the Fun Fact. Then answer the questions. 🔊 86

1. When did movies first get sound?

2. Where do you like to watch movies? In a theater? At home? Why?

Think, Pair, Share
What was the last movie you watched? What did you think about it?

Get Ready to Listen

Let's learn the **key words**.

A Listen, point, and say. Write the words in your picture dictionary. 87

adventure movie   camera operator   comedy   make a movie   radio   the news

B Listen and draw lines.  88

Max   Clare   Jane   Steve

C Listen and write. 89

1. _____ 2. _____ 3. _____

4. _____ 5. _____ 6. _____

Listen

LISTENING GOAL: Listen for Unknown Words
Sometimes there are words you don't know. When you listen, think about the words before and after the word you don't know. They can help you guess the meaning of unknown words.

A **Listen. Choose the correct answer.** 🔊 90

1. **First time / Tomorrow** helps you understand *premiere*.

2. **The United States / Made the movie** helps you understand *studio*.

3. **Actors / Dangerous** helps you understand *stunts*.

Clearview Park

B **Listen to the story *Clearview Park*. What is it about? Choose the correct picture.** 🔊 91

Now put the sentences in order.

a. Zoe heard something interesting on the radio. ☐

b. Zoe saw her favorite actor. ☐

c. Zoe went to Clearview Park. ☐

What **unknown words** did you hear?

Think!
Who is your favorite actor?
Why do you like him or her?

Understand

A Think about **Clearview Park**. What words help you understand *scene*?

☐ a. *the news, funny, adventure movie*

☐ b. *actor, lights, camera operators*

B Listen to **Clearview Park** again. Choose the correct answer. 92

1. In the car, Zoe heard the news on **the radio** / **her phone**.

2. James Tan is **a singer** / **an actor**.

3. Zoe **is** / **isn't** a big fan of James Tan.

4. The camera operators are **watching** / **making** a movie.

5. Zoe wants to take a photo with the **director** / **actor**.

C Listen. Complete each sentence with a key word. Then match. 93

1. Zoe was excited to see them _____ in her town.

2. In the park, Zoe saw many _____

3. Zoe doesn't really like _____

4. Zoe and her mom listened to the _____

a. _____

b. _____

c. _____

d. _____

D Listen to **Clearview Park** again. Work with a partner.
Complete the diagram. 🔊 94

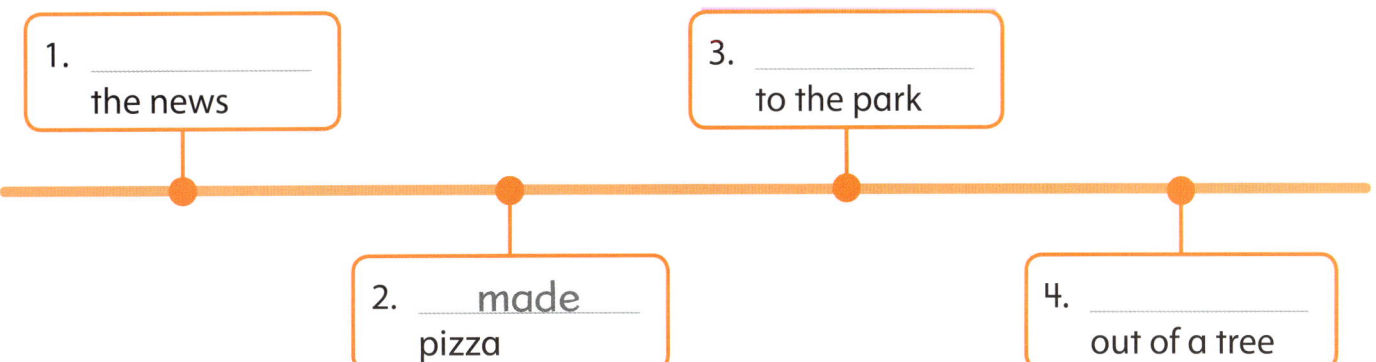

1. _____
   the news

2. ___made___
   pizza

3. _____
   to the park

4. _____
   out of a tree

E Look at **D**. Complete the sentences.

1.

They _____
_____ on the radio.

2.
He _____ made pizza.
_____

3.

She _____
_____

4.

He _____
_____

MY LISTENING GOALS

☐ I can listen to the story.

☐ I can listen for unknown words.

Get Ready to Listen

Let's learn the **key words**.

A Listen, point, and say. Write the words in your picture dictionary. 95

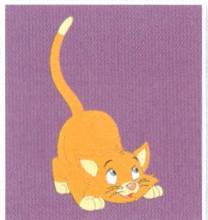     

cartoon   **documentary**   **game show**   **scary movie**   **science fiction movie**   **wildlife movie**

B Listen and number. 🔊 96

C Listen and complete the sentences. 🔊 97

1. He wants to watch a _____ , but she prefers a _____

2. Let's watch a _____ today.

3. Turn on the TV. The _____ is starting.

4. I never watch _____ or _____

Listen

LISTENING GOAL: Listen for Definitions

A definition is the meaning of a word. Listen for words like *is* or *means* to know the meaning of words.

A **Listen and number.** 🔊 98

The Weekend

B **Listen to the conversation *The Weekend*. What is it about? Choose the correct picture.** 🔊 99

A

B

Now read. Choose ✔ or ✘.

1. Kim and Paul are talking about next weekend. ✔ ✘

2. They both watched the same movie. ✔ ✘

3. Paul describes the story of a science fiction movie. ✔ ✘

Think!
Do you like watching science fiction movies? Why or why not?

How many **definitions** did you hear?

Understand

A Think about **The Weekend**.
What definitions did Kim and Paul give?
Choose **Yes** or **No**.

1. Kim gave a definition of an animal from Australia.   **Yes**   **No**

2. Paul explained what the word *planet* means.   **Yes**   **No**

B Listen to **The Weekend** again. Choose the correct answer. 🔊 100

1. Who was sick on the weekend?

☐ a. Kim   ☐ b. Paul

2. Who watched a wildlife movie?

☐ a. Kim   ☐ b. Paul

3. Who went to the movie theater?

☐ a. Kim   ☐ b. Paul

C Listen and choose the correct picture. Then write the key word. 🔊 101

1.

☐ a.   ☐ b.

2.

☐ a.   ☐ b.

3.

☐ a.   ☐ b.

4.

☐ a.   ☐ b.

D Listen to **The Weekend** again. Work with a partner.
Complete the table. 🔊 102

Kim's weekend	1. <u>stayed home</u> because she was sick
	2. watched cartoons and a _____ movie
Paul's weekend	3. went to the _____
	4. watched a _____ movie

E Look at **D**. Write the questions. Use *where* or *what*.

1.

<u>Where did Kim go?</u>
Nowhere. She stayed home.

2.

She watched a lot of TV.

3.

_____
He went to the movies.

4.

_____
He watched *Mystery Planet*.

MY LISTENING GOALS

☐ I can listen to the conversation.

☐ I can listen for definitions.

Listening Check

A **Listen to the story TV Time! What is it about? Choose the correct picture.** 🔊 103

A ☐

B ☐

C ☐

B **Which words help you understand the word *crib*? Choose ✔ or ✘.**

1. watch TV   ✔ ✘
2. sofa   ✔ ✘
3. bed   ✔ ✘
4. sleep   ✔ ✘

C **What's a *lullaby*? Choose ✔ or ✘.**

1. a song for babies   ✔ ✘
2. a movie for children   ✔ ✘
3. a bedtime song   ✔ ✘
4. a story with monsters   ✔ ✘

1. Who went out?

☐ a. Amy ☐ b. Alan ☐ c. their parents

2. What was Alan watching on TV?

☐ a. a cartoon ☐ b. a comedy ☐ c. a documentary

3. What was the scary movie about?

☐ a. an animal ☐ b. a monster ☐ c. a boy

4. Where did Amy go after turning off the TV?

☐ a. the kitchen ☐ b. her bedroom ☐ c. Alan's bedroom

5. Where was Alan?

☐ a. in his crib ☐ b. under his crib ☐ c. behind his crib

E Listen to **TV Time!** again. Complete the sentences. 🔊 105

"Bye!" Amy waved goodbye as her parents drove off that Friday night. She went back inside to her baby brother. "Alan, no more

(1) _____! Time for bed," Amy said. She took him to his crib to

sleep. "Do you want a lullaby?" she asked. "*Lullaby* means a bedtime

song for babies like you," she said. Amy sang and Alan closed his eyes.

"Goodnight, Alan."

"Now, time for TV. Finally!" Amy jumped on the sofa.

"(2) _____, no! (3) _____ or a (4) _____? Maybe.

(5) _____? I don't think so. Aha! A (6) _____. Great!" Amy

liked this kind of movie. This one was about a small boy playing in his

bedroom. Suddenly, there was a loud sound and the boy was gone.

"Ah!" Amy turned off the TV. She ran upstairs to check on Alan, but he

wasn't there. "Oh, no! It's like the movie!" Amy thought. Then she saw

a little leg under the crib. "Come here, Alan! You scared me!" she said.

Get Ready to Speak

SPEAKING GOAL: Give a Review

To give a review of a movie, describe the main characters and the plot. Don't say how it ends. Give examples to explain why you like it or don't like it.

A Read and listen to the review. Underline the examples. 🔊 106

Speaking Tip
Use phrases like *for example* or *for instance* to give examples.

The Best Adventure Movie by George Woods

The Driver is an exciting adventure movie about a taxi driver named Tom. He meets and helps a lot of different people. For instance, a police officer gets in the taxi and asks Tom to help him catch a bad man. It's also a comedy. In one scene, for example, Tom wears funny clothes and makes a sad woman happy. It's really my favorite movie because it's both exciting and funny!

B Look at **A**. George describes the movie. Complete the diagram.

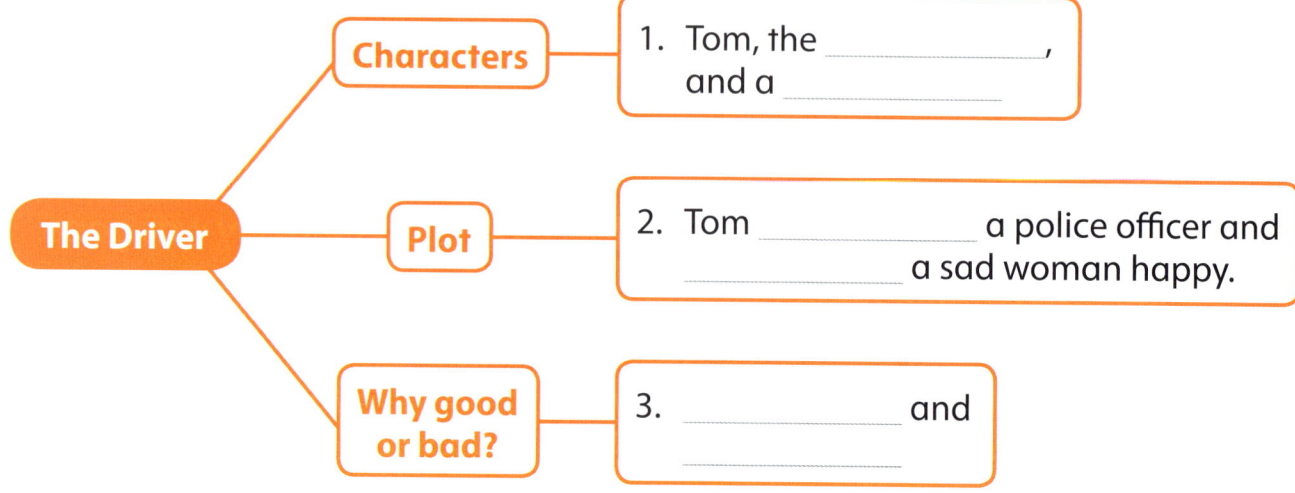

The Driver

Characters — 1. Tom, the _____, and a _____

Plot — 2. Tom _____ a police officer and _____ a sad woman happy.

Why good or bad? — 3. _____ and _____

Speak

C Think about a movie you watched. Complete the diagram.

```
                    ┌──────────────┐      ┌────────────────────────────┐
                    │  Characters  │──────│                            │
                    └──────────────┘      └────────────────────────────┘
┌──────────────┐      ┌──────────┐        ┌────────────────────────────┐
│              │──────│   Plot   │────────│                            │
└──────────────┘      └──────────┘        └────────────────────────────┘
                    ┌──────────────┐      ┌────────────────────────────┐
                    │  Why good    │──────│                            │
                    │  or bad?     │      └────────────────────────────┘
                    └──────────────┘
```

D Now write a review. Use your ideas from **C**. Choose new words, too. Then draw a picture of the movie.

_____ is a _____ movie!

The characters are _____.

They _____.

I _____ the movie because

_____.

For example, _____.

For instance, _____.

It's a _____ movie!

With your partner, tell each other your movie reviews. Do you want to see your partner's movie? Why or why not?

MY SPEAKING GOAL

☐ I can give a review.

On the Road

MY GOALS

UNIT 11

- Listen to the story *The Map*
- Identify cause and effect

UNIT 12

- Listen to the conversation *Drive to Smallville*
- Compare and contrast

SPEAK

- Give an explanation

A Look at the picture. What do you see?

1. Where are the people going?
2. Do you have roads like this where you live?

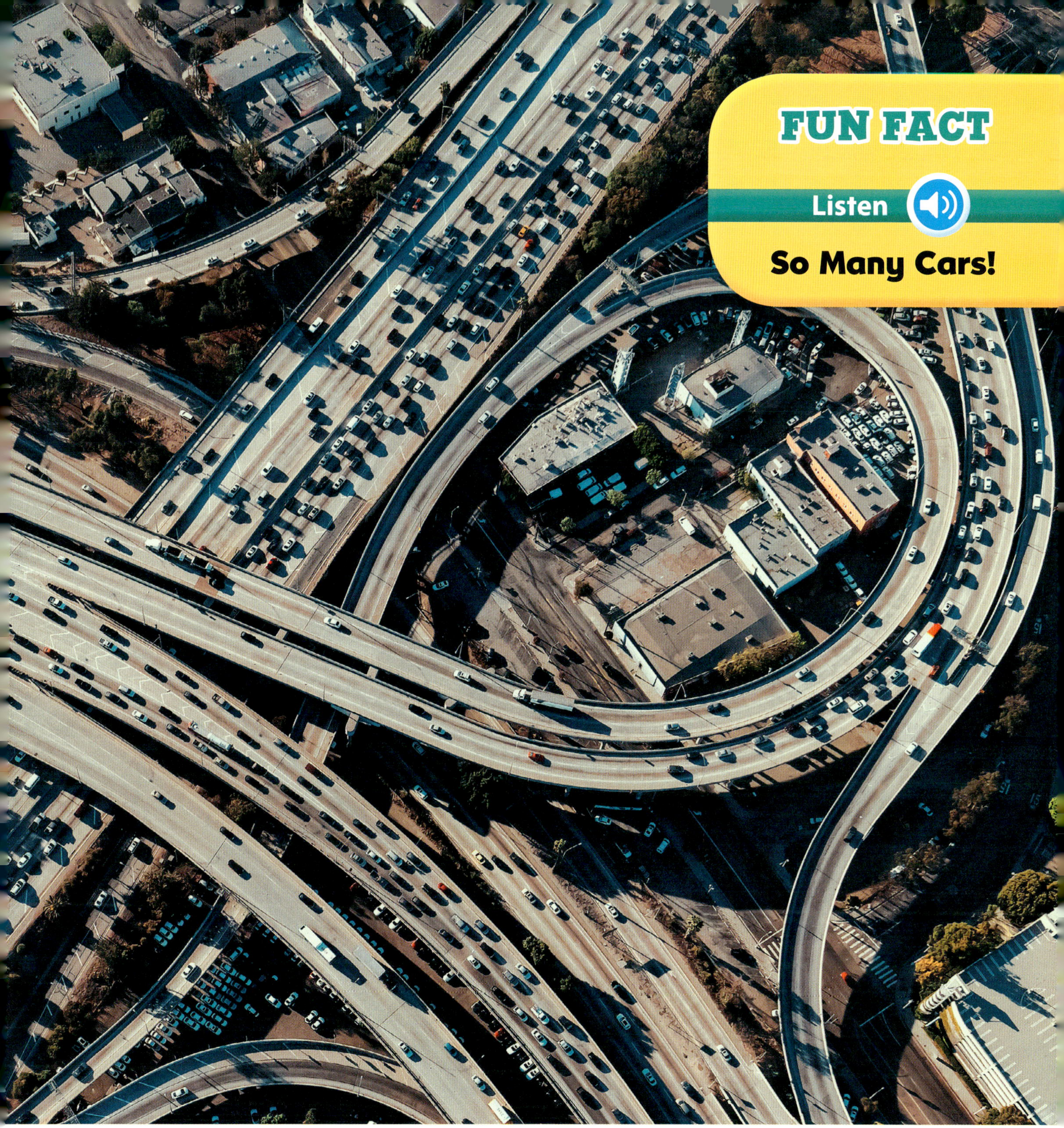

FUN FACT

Listen

So Many Cars!

B **Listen to the Fun Fact. Then answer the questions.** 107

1. What is a highway?
2. How much time do you spend in a car every day?

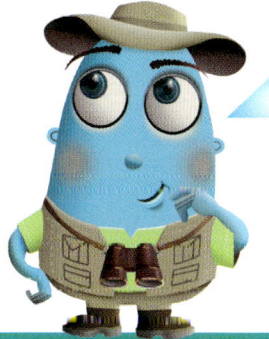

Think, Pair, Share
When was the last time you were in a car? Where did you go and why?

Get Ready to Listen

Let's learn the **key words**.

A Listen, point, and say. Write the words in your picture dictionary. 108

building

crossroads

get lost

traffic

traffic lights

van

B Listen and draw lines. 109

Vicky   Julia   Fred   Dan

C Listen and write. 110

1. _____   2. _____   3. _____

4. _____   5. _____   6. _____

Listen

A cause is why something happens. An effect is what happens because of the cause.
Listen for words like *because*, *so*, and *if* to identify causes and effects.

A **Listen. Underline the cause. Circle the effect.** 🔊 111

1. They were late because there was traffic.

2. The van didn't have any gas, so she didn't go for a drive.

3. If he doesn't stop at the traffic lights, the police can stop him.

The Map

B **Listen to the story *The Map*. What is it about?**
Choose the correct picture. 🔊 112

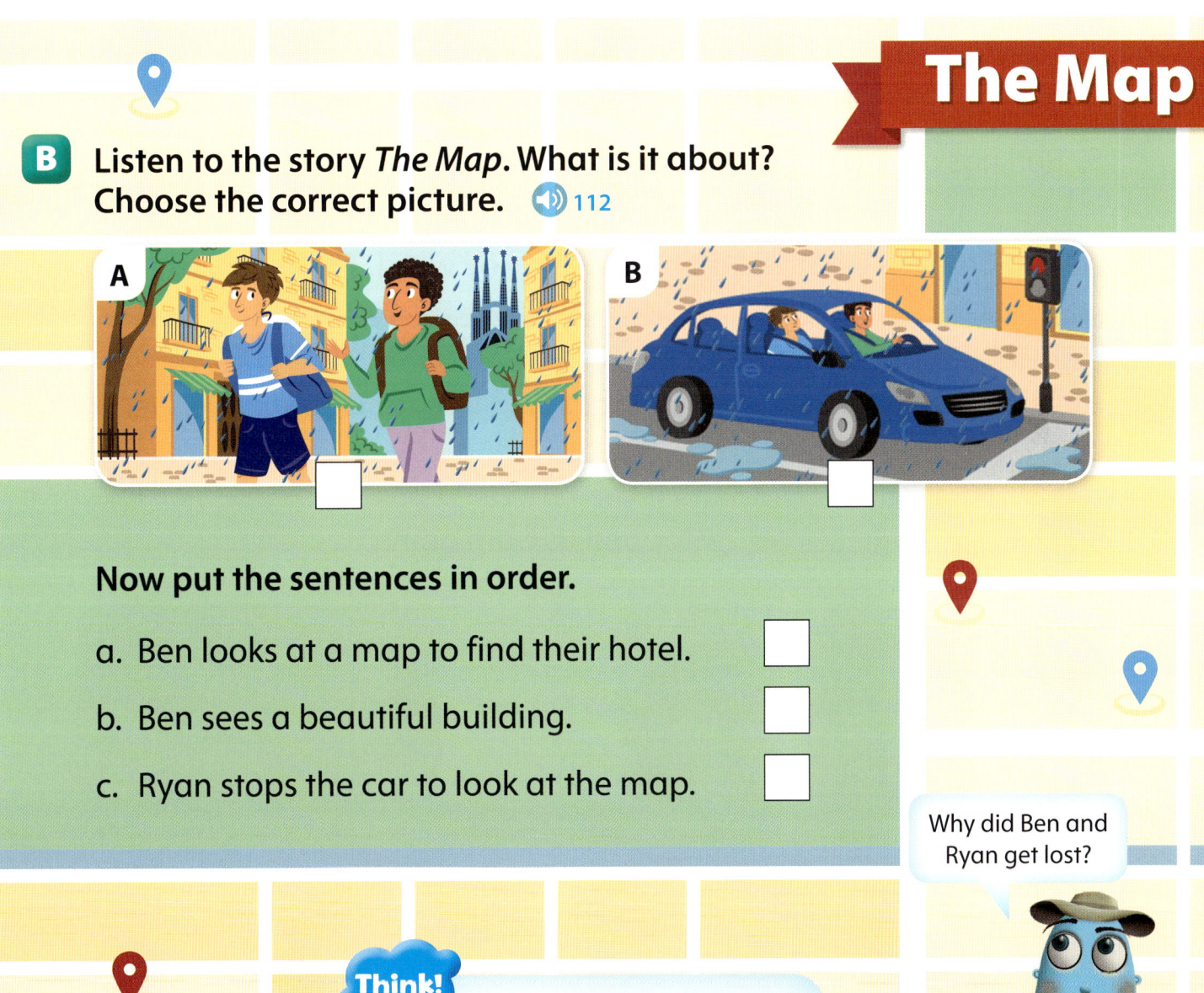

Now put the sentences in order.

a. Ben looks at a map to find their hotel.

b. Ben sees a beautiful building.

c. Ryan stops the car to look at the map.

Why did Ben and Ryan get lost?

Think!

• What can you see on a map?

Understand

A Think about **The Map**. Read the sentences. Choose **Cause** or **Effect**.

1. The friends got lost.   **Cause**   **Effect**
2. The friends had the wrong map.   **Cause**   **Effect**

B Listen to **The Map** again. Choose the correct answer. 🔊 113

1. Ben and Ryan arrive in Barcelona on **Tuesday / Wednesday**.
2. There's a lot of traffic because it's **raining / snowing**.
3. They're driving a **van / car** on their vacation.
4. They didn't turn **left / right** at the crossroads.
5. Ben has a map of **Barcelona / Badalona** on his phone.

C Listen. Complete each sentence with a key word. Then match. 🔊 114

1. There's a _____ before you get to my school.
2. I saw Peter at the _____ at Park Street and South Avenue.
3. The _____ is at the end of the street.
4. The _____ stopped us from going.

a. _____

b. _____

c. _____

d. _____

D Listen to **The Map** again. Work with a partner. Complete the diagram. 🔊 115

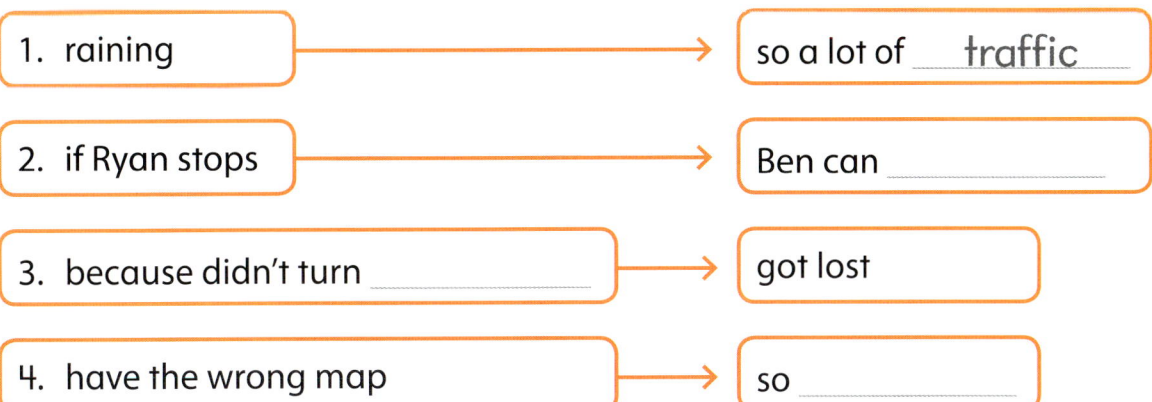

1. raining ⟶ so a lot of ___traffic___

2. if Ryan stops ⟶ Ben can _____

3. because didn't turn _____ ⟶ got lost

4. have the wrong map ⟶ so _____

E Look at **D**. Complete the sentences.

1.

It's raining, so __there's a lot of__ __traffic.__

2.

If Ryan stops, then _____
_____

3.

They got lost because _____
_____

4.

They have the wrong map, so _____
_____

MY LISTENING GOALS

☐ I can listen to the story.

☐ I can identify cause and effect.

Get Ready to Listen

Let's learn the **key words**.

A Listen, point, and say. Write the words in your picture dictionary. 116

| crowded | farm | farmers' market | motorcycle | town | truck |

B Listen and number. 117

C Listen and complete the sentences.  118

1. We're going to visit a _____ tomorrow that's near our _____

2. There's a big _____ outside our house.

3. Eric went to the _____ yesterday, and it was _____

4. When I'm older, I want to have a _____

Listen

LISTENING GOAL: Compare and Contrast

When you have two or more things, you can compare and contrast them. To compare, identify what is similar. To contrast, identify what is different. Listen for *both*, *too*, and *like* to compare. Listen for *but*, *not*, and *unlike* to contrast.

A Listen. Do the sentences compare or contrast? Choose the correct answer. 🔊 119

1. ☐ a. compare ☐ b. contrast
2. ☐ a. compare ☐ b. contrast
3. ☐ a. compare ☐ b. contrast

Drive to Smallville

B Listen to the conversation *Drive to Smallville*. What is it about? Choose the correct picture. 🔊 120

A

B

Now read. Choose ✔ or ✘.

What things do George and Sarah **compare** and **contrast**?

1. Sarah and George are making plans for next Sunday. ✔ ✘

2. They are going to go to another town. ✔ ✘

3. They are going to go with George's dad. ✔ ✘

Think!

• What are your plans for next weekend?

Understand

A Think about **Drive to Smallville**. Read the sentences. Choose the correct answer.

1. Sarah is **comparing** / **contrasting** Smallville and her town.

2. George is **comparing** / **contrasting** green and red apples.

B Listen to **Drive to Smallville** again. Choose the correct answer. 🔊 121

1. What are they going to buy at the farmers' market?
   ☐ a. vegetables   ☐ b. fruit

2. What time are they going to leave?
   ☐ a. eight o'clock   ☐ b. nine o'clock

3. How are they going to get there?
   ☐ a. in a truck   ☐ b. on a motorcycle

C Listen and choose the correct picture. Then write the key word. 🔊 122

1. ☐ a.   ☐ b.   2. ☐ a.   ☐ b.

3. ☐ a.   ☐ b.   4. ☐ a.   ☐ b.

D Listen to **Drive to Smallville** again. Work with a partner. Complete the diagram. 🔊 123

1. go to a __farmers' market__

2. buy _____

Next Saturday, we are going to

3. leave at _____

4. take the _____

E Look at **D**. Write. Use *be going to*.

1.

We __are going to go to__ __a farmers' market.__

2.

We _____

_____

3.

We _____

_____

4.

We _____

_____

MY LISTENING GOALS

☐ I can listen to the conversation.

☐ I can listen to compare and contrast.

Listening Check

Remember!
Listen for **causes** and **effects**. What happens and why? Listen to **compare** and **contrast**. How are things similar and different?

A Listen to the interview **World Travelers**. What is it about? Choose the correct picture. 🔊 124

 A

 B

 C

B What causes and effects are in the interview? Choose ✔ or ✘.

1. They're traveling by car, so traffic isn't a problem.

2. If they get lost, they stop and ask for help.

3. Mike enjoys big cities, so they never stay in towns.

4. They work because they need money for the trip.

C What does the interview compare and contrast? Choose ✔ or ✘.

1. Both Cindy and Mike love cars.

2. Mike chooses towns, but Cindy chooses cities.

3. Small towns are crowded like cities.

4. Both Cindy and Mike's favorite animals are horses.

1. Where are Cindy and Mike traveling?
   - ☐ a. around Europe
   - ☐ b. around the US
   - ☐ c. around the world

2. What does Cindy like about traveling on the motorcycle?
   - ☐ a. the wind
   - ☐ b. the rain
   - ☐ c. the sun

3. How often do Cindy and Mike get lost?
   - ☐ a. never
   - ☐ b. always
   - ☐ c. sometimes

4. What kind of towns does Mike like?
   - ☐ a. busy
   - ☐ b. small
   - ☐ c. crowded

E Listen to **World Travelers** again. Complete the sentences. 🔊 126

Ian: Hello, Cindy. You and your brother, Mike, are traveling around the world on your (1) _____. Why don't you travel by car?

Cindy: We both love motorcycles. They're more fun. I enjoy feeling the wind, and (2) _____ isn't a problem.

Ian: You're in China now. Do you ever (3) _____?

Cindy: Yes! We use maps on our phones. Sometimes our phones don't work though, so we get lost. If we get lost, we stop and ask for help.

Ian: Where do you stay?

Cindy: Well, I love to stay in big cities, unlike Mike. He always chooses small (4) _____ because they're not (5) _____ like cities. And it's easier to find work there.

Ian: Why do you work?

Cindy: We work because we have to make money to pay for our trip. Next week, we're going to work with animals on a (6) _____.

Ian: Wow, that's great! What kind of animals?

Cindy: Horses! They're my favorite animal, and Mike's favorite, too!

Get Ready to Speak

SPEAKING GOAL: Give an Explanation

To give an explanation, describe how you do something, how to make something, or how something works.

A Read and listen to the explanation. Underline the steps. 🔊 127

Speaking Tip
Use words like *first*, *second*, *third*, and *fourth* to explain how.

Tim: Look. I made this toy motorcycle.

Ann: Wow! How did you make that?

Tim: First, I checked that I had all the pieces, so I counted them. Second, I cleaned and dried them. Third, I painted everything. And fourth, I used a very strong glue to put all the pieces together.

Ann: It's great!

B Look at **A**. What are the steps? Complete the diagram.

How to Make a Toy Motorcycle

1. First	2. Second	3. Third	4. Fourth
_____	_____	_____	_____
_____	_____	_____	_____
_____		_____	

Speak

C Think about something you did or made. How do you explain it? Complete the diagram.

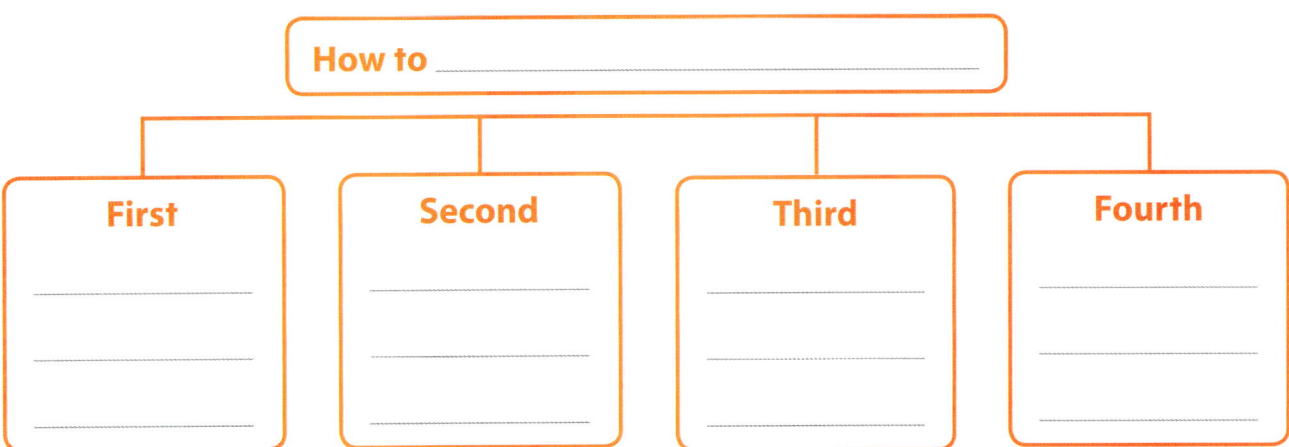

How to _____

First	Second	Third	Fourth
_____	_____	_____	_____
_____	_____	_____	_____
_____	_____	_____	_____

D Now write your explanation. Use your ideas from **C**. Use *first*, *second*, *third*, and *fourth*. Then draw a picture of what you did or made.

I _____

First, _____

Second, _____

Third, _____

And fourth, _____

 Work with a partner. Give an explanation for the thing you did or made. Then ask your partner to give his or her explanation.

MY SPEAKING GOAL

☐ I can give an explanation.

Listening with Speaking 4

Workbook

Katie Foufouti

OXFORD
UNIVERSITY PRESS

Listen

LISTENING GOAL:
Listen for the Topic

Remember!
Listen for the **topic**. It's what the listening is about, and the speaker usually says it in the first or second sentence.

A Listen to the passage **The Grand to Grand Ultra**. What do you hear about? Choose ✔ or ✘. 🔊 128

1.

swimmers ✔ ✘

2.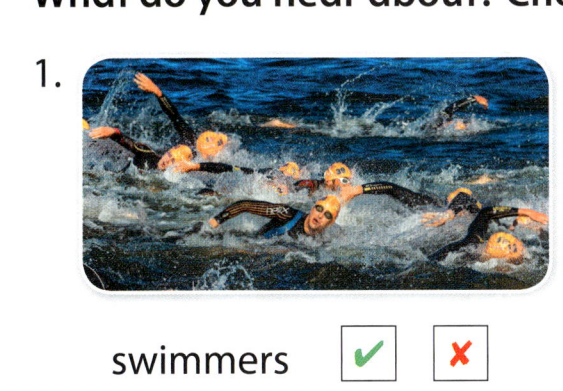

runners ✔ ✘

B Think about **The Grand to Grand Ultra**. What is the topic? Choose ✔ or ✘.

1. last year's winner of the race   ✔   ⊗
2. how difficult the race is   ✔   ✘
3. how to get ready for the race   ✔   ✘

C Listen to **The Grand to Grand Ultra** again. Choose the correct answer. 🔊 129

1. Where does this race take place?
   ☐ a. Australia   ☐ b. the UK   ✔ c. the United States

2. How many days does the race take to run?
   ☐ a. 7   ☐ b. 17   ☐ c. 70

3. How many kilometers is it?
   ☐ a. 237   ☐ b. 273   ☐ c. 723

4. When is the race this year?
   ☐ a. September   ☐ b. October   ☐ c. November

D Listen and write the key word. Then choose the correct picture. 🔊 130

1. _____ oasis _____

2. _____

✔ a.   ☐ b.

☐ a.   ☐ b.

3. _____

4. _____

☐ a.   ☐ b.

☐ a.   ☐ b.

E Complete the sentences.

| pond | temperature | canyon | desert | ~~stream~~ | oasis |

1. The _____ stream _____ is long and goes through the field and forest.

2. There's a _____ with ducks near his house.

3. The _____ on Friday is going to be 20–25 degrees.

4. There aren't many plants in the _____

F Unscramble and write.

1. p a t u e e r t m r e

_____ temperature _____

2. s o i a s

_____

3. n c a o n y

_____

4. s a e r m t

_____

Listen

LISTENING GOAL:
Listen for the Main Idea and Details

Remember!
The **main idea** helps you understand the topic. The **details** give you more information about the main idea.

A Listen to the story **Behind the Waterfall**. Then put the pictures in order. 🔊 131

A

Climb up here!

[ ]

B

1

C

[ ]

B Think about **Behind the Waterfall**. Choose ✔ or ✗.

1. "An adventure on Candy Island" is the main idea.   ✔ ✗

2. "Kate found a cave" is a detail.   ✔ ✗

3. "Kate was scared to go inside the cave" is a detail.   ✔ ✗

C Listen to **Behind the Waterfall** again. Choose Yes or No. 🔊 132

1. Many people visit Candy Island.   **Yes** **(No)**

2. Kate travels to Candy Island every summer.   **Yes** **No**

3. There isn't a cliff on Candy Island.   **Yes** **No**

4. Last year, Kate and Scott found a waterfall.   **Yes** **No**

5. Kate climbed up to the waterfall.   **Yes** **No**

6. There was somebody inside the cave.   **Yes** **No**

D Listen. Then read and choose the correct answer. 🔊 133

1. Where did the brothers go?

a.    b.    c.

2. What did the boy see?

a.    b.    c.

3. Where is the girl?

a.    b.    c.

E Complete the sentences.

1. There are crocodiles in this r_____

2. Don't go too close to the edge of the c_____

3. We take a ferry to get to the i_____

4. Niagara Falls is a big w_____ in Canada and the United States.

Speak

> **Remember!**
> Words with similar meanings are called *synonyms*. Use them to paraphrase.

Circle the synonyms in the sentences. Then think of your own sentences with synonyms. Tell your partner.

The beaches are beautiful. The island is so pretty.

My dad is a great cook. He works as a chef.

The cave was frightening. It was so scary.

Listen

LISTENING GOAL:
Listen and Take Notes —
Split Page

Remember!
When you take **split-page notes**, write the main ideas on the left and the details on the right.

A Listen to the interview **A Young Sports Star**. Take notes. 🔊 134

Main Ideas	Details

B Think about **A Young Sports Star** and look at your notes. Which main idea is the detail "we like golf and soccer" about? Choose ✔ or ✘.

1. Meg plays other sports, too.   ✔   ✘

2. Meg and her mom watch sports on TV.   ✔   ✘

3. Meg is very good at tennis.   ✔   ✘

C Listen to **A Young Sports Star** again. Choose the correct answer. 🔊 135

1. What kind of tournament did Meg win?
   ☐ a. table tennis   ☐ b. tennis   ☐ c. golf

2. How many days a week does Meg practice tennis?
   ☐ a. five   ☐ b. two   ☐ c. four

3. What sport does Meg play at school?
   ☐ a. volleyball   ☐ b. tennis   ☐ c. table tennis

4. What sport does Meg like to watch on TV?
   ☐ a. golf   ☐ b. volleyball   ☐ c. table tennis

D Listen and write the key word. Then choose the correct picture. 🔊 136

1. _____

☐ a.   ☐ b.

2. _____

☐ a.   ☐ b.

3. _____

☐ a.   ☐ b.

4. _____

☐ a.   ☐ b.

E Complete the sentences.

| play volleyball | play tennis | play table tennis |
| play golf | coach | practice tai chi |

1. I _____. I can jump high.

2. You and my _____ _____ at the same golf course.

3. We have a new table to _____.

F Unscramble and write.

1. a l y p   o l v l y b l e a l

   _____

2. l p y a   t i s n e n

   _____

3. c i e a c t p r   a t i   i c h

   _____

4. y p a l   b t l a e   n e i n s t

   _____

Listen

LISTENING GOAL:
Listen and Make Predictions

A Listen to the story **A New Club at Rose School**.
Then put the pictures in order. 🔊 137

A

B

C

B Think about **A New Club at Rose School**. What's going to happen?
Choose ✔ or ✘.

1. Jesse is going to make new friends.   ✔   ✘

2. Jesse is going to get better at sports.   ✔   ✘

3. Jesse is going to stop playing chess.   ✔   ✘

C Listen to **A New Club at Rose School** again. Choose Yes or No. 🔊 138

1. Most students at Rose School like to play sports.   **Yes   No**

2. Jesse is good at math, but he doesn't like sports.   **Yes   No**

3. Many children at Rose School play chess.   **Yes   No**

4. Mrs. Castle is going to teach children to play chess.   **Yes   No**

5. Mrs. Castle tells Jesse about her idea.   **Yes   No**

6. Jesse likes Mrs. Castle's idea about the new club.   **Yes   No**

D Listen. Then read and choose the correct answer. 🔊 139

1. What sport is the boy watching?

a.    b.    c.

2. Which sport did the girl win a trophy for?

a.    b.    c.

3. What does the boy want to learn?

a.    b.    c.

E Complete the sentences.

1. Congratulations! You w_____ the t_____

2. Let's go to the beach. I can teach you how to s_____

3. Every morning, Mike j_____ in the park.

4. We d_____ g_____ at the sports center.

Remember!
Use *be going to* when you make predictions.

Speak

Underline the information that helps Ed make a prediction. Think of your own story. Tell your partner.

It's Ed's turn in the gymnastics tournament. "Ouch!" he says, and holds his knee. His coach looks worried. "I'm not going to win," Ed tells him.

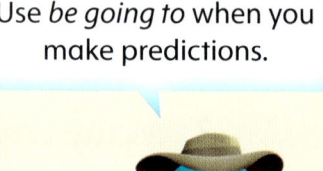

Listen

LISTENING GOAL:
Listen for Facts and Opinions

A Listen to the conversation **My Cousin Fred**. What do you hear about? Choose ✔ or ✘. 🔊 140

1.

a day at the museum ✔ ✘

2.

a day at the zoo ✔ ✘

B Think about **My Cousin Fred**. Are the sentences facts or opinions? Choose **F** for fact or **O** for opinion.

1. Meg and Fred are cousins.   **F O**

2. Fred's hair is brown.   **F O**

3. Fred has pretty eyes.   **F O**

C Listen to **My Cousin Fred** again. Choose the correct answer. 🔊 141

1. Who got lost in the zoo?
   ☐ a. Meg   ☐ b. Fred   ☐ c. Meg's aunt

2. What does Fred's hair look like?
   ☐ a. straight   ☐ b. curly   ☐ c. wavy

3. What is he wearing that's black?
   ☐ a. a cap   ☐ b. a T-shirt   ☐ c. sneakers

4. What animals was Fred looking at before he got lost?
   ☐ a. penguins   ☐ b. crocodiles   ☐ c. elephants

D Listen and write the key word. Then choose the correct picture. 🔊 142

1. _____

2. _____

☐ a.   ☐ b.

☐ a.   ☐ b.

3. _____

4. _____

☐ a.   ☐ b.

☐ a.   ☐ b.

E Complete the sentences.

| kind   wavy hair   eyebrows   cry   skin   dark |

1. I'm so sad. I think I'm going to _____

2. Can you move your _____ up and down?

3. My dad has short, _____

4. He has a _____ beard, too.

F Unscramble and write.

1. k s n i

2. r d k a

_____

_____

3. i n d k

4. c y r

_____

_____

Listen

LISTENING GOAL:
Listen for Plot

A Listen to the story **Prince Rob Enzel**. Then put the pictures in order. 🔊 143

B Think about **Prince Rob Enzel**. What happens in each part of the plot? Choose ✔ or ✘.

1. **Beginning:** You hear about Rob and a little girl.   ✔ ✘

2. **Middle:** The problem is that Rob can't leave the castle.   ✔ ✘

3. **End:** The solution is that King John lets Rob go.   ✔ ✘

C Listen to **Prince Rob Enzel** again. Choose **Yes** or **No**. 🔊 144

1. King John was Rob's father.   **Yes**   **No**

2. King John wanted to win at chess.   **Yes**   **No**

3. Rob couldn't leave his uncle's castle.   **Yes**   **No**

4. Rob got a haircut while he was locked in the castle.   **Yes**   **No**

5. The girl saw Rob's beard first, and then she saw Rob.   **Yes**   **No**

6. The girl climbed up Rob's hair to get to the top.   **Yes**   **No**

D Listen. Then read and choose the correct answer. 🔊 145

1. What is the girl going to do?

a. 　　b. 　　c.

2. Who's Danielle?

a. 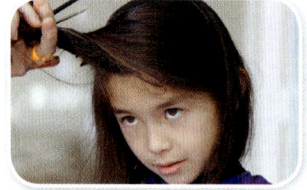　　b. 　　c.

3. Who's Sally?

a. 　　b. 　　c.

E Complete the sentences.

1. I'm going to g _____ a h _____ tomorrow.

2. I wear my hair in a b _____ to play volleyball.

3. Grace is very c _____. She's good at math and science.

4. Mom, where are my e _____

> **Remember!**
> Use *I think* and *In my opinion* to give your opinion. Use *What do you think?* to ask for opinions.

Speak

Underline the opinion phrases. Then think of your own sentences with opinions. Tell your partner and ask for his or her opinion.

I think Tim is very funny because he tells good jokes. What do you think?

In my opinion, the restaurant is great because it has the best burgers. What do you think?

Listen

LISTENING GOAL:
Listen for Reactions

Remember!
You can tell a person's feelings from his or her **reactions** after something happens.

A Listen to the story **Breakfast in Bed**. What do you hear about? Choose ✔ or ✘. 🔊 146

1.

waking up on Earth   ✔ ✘

2.

waking up in space   ✔ ✘

B Think about **Breakfast in Bed**. How do the characters react? Choose ✔ or ✘.

1. Leyla said, "What's all this?" because she was surprised.   ✔ ✘

2. Leyla laughed because Michael told a funny story.   ✔ ✘

3. Leyla said, "Oh, no!" because she didn't like the coffee.   ✔ ✘

C Listen to **Breakfast in Bed** again. Choose the correct answer. 🔊 147

1. Leyla didn't want to wake up because
   ☐ a. her bed was nice.
   ☐ b. it was raining.
   ☐ c. she didn't want to work.

2. How long did Leyla stay in space?
   ☐ a. four months
   ☐ b. five months
   ☐ c. six months

3. Who are Eva and Michael?
   ☐ a. Leyla's friends
   ☐ b. Leyla's children
   ☐ c. Leyla's parents

4. What's the problem with Leyla?
   ☐ a. She's too tired.
   ☐ b. She's sick.
   ☐ c. She's not strong.

D Listen and write the key word. Then choose the correct picture. 🔊 148

1. _____

☐ a.   ☐ b.

2. _____

☐ a.   ☐ b.

3. _____

☐ a.   ☐ b.

4. _____

☐ a.   ☐ b.

E Complete the sentences.

| planet | galaxy | land | ground | meteorite | footprint |

1. What time does the plane _____

2. My favorite _____ is Mars.

3. This is where a big _____ crashed.

4. I found this key on the _____. Whose is it?

F Unscramble and write.

1. r m e t o i t e e

_____

2. u g n d r o

_____

3. a l x g y a

_____

4. o r i o t p n f t

_____

Listen

LISTENING GOAL:
Listen for Tone

Remember!
The way a person talks helps you understand how he or she feels.

A Listen to the class presentations **When I'm Older**. Then put the pictures in order. 🔊 149

A

B

C

B Think about **When I'm Older**. How do the children feel? Choose ✔ or ✗.

1. They talk slowly because they're bored. ✔ ✗

2. They talk quickly because they're excited. ✔ ✗

3. They talk quietly because they're afraid. ✔ ✗

C Listen to **When I'm Older** again. Choose Yes or No. 🔊 150

1. Paul wants to take care of small animals.   **Yes**   **No**

2. Paul wants to work in a zoo.   **Yes**   **No**

3. Jenny wants to build bridges in the future.   **Yes**   **No**

4. Jenny is good at drawing and science.   **Yes**   **No**

5. Kadir isn't interested In space.   **Yes**   **No**

6. Kadir wants to write books.   **Yes**   **No**

D Listen. Then read and choose the correct answer. 🔊 151

1. What are the girl and her friend watching?

a.
b.
c.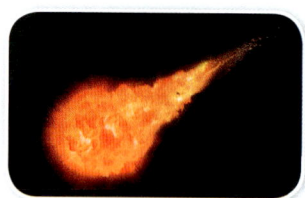

2. What is the man reading about?

a.
b.
c.

3. What is the woman looking at?

a.
b.
c.

E Complete the sentences.

1. Joon-Won's d_____ is to become an astronaut.

2. I can see the m_____ from my bedroom window.

3. They sent a s_____ to space to take photos of Earth.

4. How many planets are there in our s_____

   s_____

Speak

Remember!
Say reaction words like *wow*, *aw*, and *oh* more loudly, quietly, quickly, or slowly to show how you feel.

Underline the reaction words. Then think of your own sentences. Tell your partner.

Oh, that sounds really scary!

Wow, that's amazing!

Listen

LISTENING GOAL:
Listen for Unknown Words

A Listen to the story **Where's the Movie?** What do you hear about?
Choose ✔ or ✘. 🔊 152

1.

a movie by students ✔ ✘

2.

a movie by teachers ✔ ✘

B Think about **Where's the Movie?** What phrases help you understand
the words? Choose ✔ or ✘.

1. *Something funny happened to Frank* helps me
   understand *roles*. ✔ ✘

2. *Grace was the writer* helps me understand *script*. ✔ ✘

3. *Is it gone?* helps me understand *delete*. ✔ ✘

C Listen to **Where's the Movie?** again. Choose the correct answer. 🔊 153

1. What kind of movie was made?
   ☐ a. a scary movie   ☐ b. a documentary   ☐ c. a comedy

2. Who was the main actor?
   ☐ a. Frank   ☐ b. Hugo   ☐ c. Grace

3. What was Mark looking for?
   ☐ a. the movie   ☐ b. his phone   ☐ c. his computer

4. How did Grace feel at the end?
   ☐ a. sad   ☐ b. angry   ☐ c. happy

D Listen and write the key word. Then choose the correct picture. 🔊 154

1. _____

☐ a.   ☐ b.

2. _____

☐ a.   ☐ b.

3. _____

☐ a.   ☐ b.

4. _____

☐ a.   ☐ b.

E Complete the sentences.

> comedy   the news   camera operator
>
> adventure movie   radio   make a movie

1. The actor wants to _____ in the desert.

2. I heard a _____ show on the _____ yesterday. It was so funny!

3. _____ is on at 12 p.m. and 9 p.m. every day.

F Unscramble and write.

1. n r e d u a t v e   o i v m e

    _____

2. m a c a e r   r o o e r p a t

    _____

3. c m o e y d

    _____

4. h t e   w e s n

    _____

WORKBOOK
UNIT 10

Listen

LISTENING GOAL:
Listen for Definitions

Remember! **Definitions** usually have the word *is* or *means*.

A Listen to the radio announcement **What to Watch**. Then put the pictures in order. 🔊 155

A

B

C

B Think about **What to Watch**. What definitions do you hear? Choose ✔ or ✘.

1. *Contestant* means a person playing in a game show.

2. *Monster* is something scary.

3. *Lynx* is a wild animal.

C Listen to **What to Watch** again. Choose Yes or No. 🔊 156

1. You can hear *What to Watch* on the radio.   **Yes   No**

2. The game show is called *100 Questions*.   **Yes   No**

3. The game show is on three times a week.   **Yes   No**

4. *Baby Monsters* starts on Wednesday.   **Yes   No**

5. *Mystery Planet* is a movie.   **Yes   No**

6. *Wild Cats* is about animals, like lions.   **Yes   No**

Unit 10 Workbook **109**

D Listen. Then read and choose the correct answer. 🔊 157

1. What did the girl watch?

a.    b.    c.

2. Which movie did the boy like?

a.    b.    c.

3. What are the friends going to watch?

a.    b.    c.

E Complete the sentences.

1. Yesterday, we watched a d_____ about our solar system.

2. Do you want to watch this w_____ about hippos?

3. Helen couldn't sleep last night because she watched a s_____

4. This c_____ is for little children. I don't like it.

Speak

Remember!
Use *for example* or *for instance* to give examples.

Underline the examples in the review. Then think of your own sentences with examples. Tell your partner.

The cartoon had lots of funny scenes. For instance, the scene in the park made me laugh. And many of the characters were great, too. For example, I really liked the cat and the dog. The cat was very clever, and the dog was very kind.

Listen

**LISTENING GOAL:
Identify Cause and Effect**

> **Remember!**
> To find a **cause** and its **effect**, listen for words like *because*, *so*, and *if*.

A Listen to the story **Around New York**. What do you hear about? Choose ✔ or ✘. 🔊 158

1.

Mary's life in New York

2.

Mary's grandfather when he was young

B Think about **Around New York**. What happened and why? Choose ✔ or ✘.

1. Mary's grandfather worked because he had to pay for school. ✔ ✘

2. He had a dangerous job because he carried heavy things. ✔ ✘

3. It was summer, so he was hot. ✔ ✘

C Listen to **Around New York** again. Choose the correct answer. 🔊 159

1. What did Mary's grandfather carry?
   ☐ a. flowers   ☐ b. bicycles   ☐ c. letters

2. What did he look at when he stopped at the traffic lights?
   ☐ a. the people   ☐ b. the buildings   ☐ c. the traffic

3. How long did he ride his bicycle until he found the office?
   ☐ a. one hour   ☐ b. two hours   ☐ c. three hours

4. Who was the young woman who opened the door?
   ☐ a. Mary's mom   ☐ b. Mary's aunt   ☐ c. Mary's grandmother

D Listen and write the key word. Then choose the correct picture. 🔊 160

1. _____

☐ a. ☐ b.

2. _____

☐ a. ☐ b.

3. _____

☐ a. ☐ b.

4. _____

☐ a. ☐ b.

E Complete the sentences.

| building | van | get lost | traffic light | traffic | crossroads |

1. The bookstore is inside that tall _____

2. Don't walk if the _____ is red.

3. Our family is big, so we have a _____

4. There's not much _____ late in the evening.

F Unscramble and write.

1. t g e   s t o l

_____

2. d i u g i l b n

_____

3. i r t f a f c   s l h t i g

_____

4. r o s a o s d s c r

_____

Listen

LISTENING GOAL:
Compare and Contrast

A Listen to the class announcement **Our Field Trip**. Then put the pictures in order. 🔊 161

B Think about **Our Field Trip**. Are the things similar or different? Choose **S** for similar or **D** for different.

1. The market is crowded on the weekend, but not on Fridays.   **S   D**

2. Both the fruits and vegetables are from farms near the town.   **S   D**

3. Cherries and peaches grow in the summer, like strawberries.   **S   D**

C Listen to **Our Field Trip** again. Choose **Yes** or **No**. 🔊 162

1. The students are going to go to the Dallas farmers' market.   **Yes   No**

2. The Northlake market is too big.   **Yes   No**

3. They're going to the farmers' market by bus.   **Yes   No**

4. They have to be at the front gate at 8:30.   **Yes   No**

5. The students can buy cherries and strawberries.   **Yes   No**

6. The students are going to make sandwiches at the market.   **Yes   No**

D Listen. Then read and choose the correct answer. 🔊 163

1. Where are the father and daughter going to go?

   a.    b.    c.

2. Where did the friends go on Sunday?

   a.    b.    c.

3. How is the man going to get to town?

   a.    b.    c.

E Complete the sentences.

1. It's really _c_____ and loud in here. Let's go!

2. Do you know how to drive a big _t_____

3. There isn't any traffic in our _t_____. That's why I like it!

4. Sometimes my aunt takes me for a ride on her _m_____

Speak

> **Remember!**
> To explain how, use step words like *first*, *second*, *third*, and *fourth*.

Underline the step words. Then think of your own sentences to explain something you did or made. Tell your partner.

First, I got out my bicycle tools.

Second, I read a book about how to fix a tire.

Third, I used my tools to fix my tire.

Picture Dictionary

Write the key words.

Unit 1

_____

_____

_____

_____

_____

_____

Unit 2

_____

_____

_____

_____

_____

_____

Unit 3

_____

_____

_____

_____

_____

_____

Unit 4

_____

_____

_____

_____

_____

_____

Picture Dictionary

Unit 5

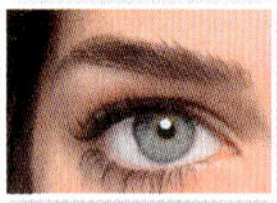

_____

_____

_____

_____

_____

_____

Unit 6

_____

_____

_____

_____

_____

_____

Unit 7

_____

_____

_____

_____

_____

_____

Unit 8

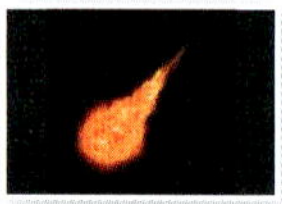

_____

_____

_____

_____

_____

_____

Unit 9

_____

_____

_____

_____

_____

_____

Unit 10

_____

_____

_____

_____

_____

_____

Unit 11

_____

_____

_____

_____

_____

_____

Unit 12

_____

_____

_____

_____

_____

_____

Syllabus

Topic	Unit	Listening Goal	Key Words	Speaking Goal
TOPIC 1 Exploring Our World	Unit 1	Listen for the topic	*canyon, desert, oasis, pond, stream, temperature*	Paraphrase
	Unit 2	Listen for the main idea and details	*canal, cave, cliff, island, river, waterfall*	Focus: Synonyms
TOPIC 2 Faster, Higher, Stronger!	Unit 3	Listen and take notes — split page	*coach, play golf, play table tennis, play tennis, play volleyball, practice tai chi*	Make predictions
	Unit 4	Listen and make predictions	*do gymnastics, do judo, jog, play chess, surf, win a trophy*	Focus: Educated guesses
TOPIC 3 Look Good! Feel Good!	Unit 5	Listen for facts and opinions	*cry, dark, eyebrows, kind, skin, wavy hair*	Give and ask for opinions
	Unit 6	Listen for plot	*angry, braid, clever, earrings, get a haircut, make jewelry*	Focus: Opinion phrases and questions
TOPIC 4 What's Out There?	Unit 7	Listen for reactions	*footprint, galaxy, ground, land, meteorite, planet*	Use tones to react
	Unit 8	Listen for tone	*asteroid, dream, moon, satellite, solar system, star*	Focus: Reaction words and phrases
TOPIC 5 What Can We Watch?	Unit 9	Listen for unknown words	*adventure movie, camera operator, comedy, make a movie, radio, the news*	Give a review
	Unit 10	Listen for definitions	*cartoon, documentary, game show, scary movie, science fiction movie, wildlife movie*	Focus: Example phrases
TOPIC 6 On the Road	Unit 11	Identify cause and effect	*building, crossroads, get lost, traffic, traffic lights, van*	Give an explanation
	Unit 12	Compare and contrast	*crowded, farm, farmers' market, motorcycle, town, truck*	Focus: Ordinal numbers